Come, Follow Me—
For Individuals and Families

Living, Learning, and Teaching the Gospel of Jesus Christ

Published by
The Church of Jesus Christ of Latter-day Saints
Salt Lake City, Utah

Published by The Church of Jesus Christ of Latter-day Saints

Contents

Conversion Is Our Goal

The aim of all gospel learning and teaching is to deepen our conversion to Heavenly Father and Jesus Christ and help us become more like Them. For this reason, when we study the gospel, we're not just looking for new information; we want to become a "new creature" (2 Corinthians 5:17). This means relying on Heavenly Father and Jesus Christ to help us change our hearts, our views, our actions, and our very natures.

But the kind of gospel learning that strengthens our faith and leads to the miracle of conversion doesn't happen all at once. It extends beyond a classroom into our hearts and homes. It requires consistent, daily efforts to understand and live the gospel. Gospel learning that leads to true conversion requires the influence of the Holy Ghost.

The Holy Ghost guides us to the truth and bears witness of that truth (see John 16:13). He enlightens our minds, quickens our understandings, and touches our hearts with revelation from God, the source of all truth. The Holy Ghost purifies our hearts. He inspires in us a desire to live by truth, and He whispers to us ways to do this. Truly, "the Holy Ghost . . . shall teach [us] all things" (John 14:26).

For these reasons, in our efforts to live, learn, and teach the gospel, we should first and foremost seek the companionship of the Spirit. This goal should govern our choices and guide our thoughts and actions. We should seek after whatever invites the influence of the Spirit and reject whatever drives that influence away—for we know that if we can be worthy of the presence of the Holy Ghost, we can also be worthy to live in the presence of Heavenly Father and His Son, Jesus Christ.

Using *Come, Follow Me—For Individuals and Families*

Who Is This Resource For?

This resource is for every individual and family in the Church. It is designed to help you learn the gospel—whether on your own or with your family. If you haven't studied the gospel regularly in the past, this resource can help you get started. If you already have a good habit of gospel study, this resource can help you have more meaningful experiences.

How Should I Use This Resource?

Use this resource in any way that is helpful to you. You may find it helpful as a guide or aid for personal and family scripture study. You could also use it for home evening. The outlines highlight important principles found in the New Testament, suggest study ideas and activities for individuals and families, and provide places to record your impressions.

Come, Follow Me—For Individuals and Families is not meant to replace or compete with other good things you are doing to learn the gospel. Follow the Spirit's guidance to determine how to approach your own study of the word of God.

How Does This Resource Relate to What Happens at Church?

The outlines in this resource are organized according to a weekly reading schedule. The *Come, Follow Me* resources for Primary, for Sunday School, and for Aaronic Priesthood quorums and Young Women classes follow the same schedule. To support your efforts to learn and live the gospel at home, your teachers at church will give you opportunities to share your experiences, thoughts, and questions about the scripture passages that you have been studying at home.

Because Sunday School is taught only twice a month, Sunday School teachers may choose to skip or combine outlines to keep up with the weekly schedule. This may also be necessary (for both Sunday School and Primary) on weeks when regular Church meetings are not held because of stake conference or other reasons. During these weeks you are invited to continue to study the New Testament at home.

Do I Need to Follow the Schedule?

The schedule will help you read the New Testament by the end of the year. In addition, following the same schedule as others can lead to meaningful experiences at home, at church, and elsewhere. But don't feel bound by the schedule or compelled to read every verse; the schedule is simply a guide to help you pace yourself. The important thing is that you are learning the gospel individually and as a family.

Ideas to Improve Your Personal Scripture Study

Here are some simple ways to enhance your study of the word of God in the scriptures.

Look for Truths about Jesus Christ

The scriptures teach us that all things testify of Christ (see 2 Nephi 11:4; Moses 6:63), so consider noting or marking verses that teach about the Savior and how to follow Him.

Look for Inspiring Words and Phrases

You may find that certain words and phrases in the scriptures impress you, as if they were written specifically for you. They may feel personally relevant and inspire and motivate you. Consider marking them in your scriptures or writing them in a study journal.

Look for Gospel Truths

Sometimes gospel truths (often called doctrine or principles) are stated directly, and sometimes they are implied through an example or story. Ask yourself, "What eternal truths are taught in these verses?"

Listen to the Spirit

Pay attention to your thoughts and feelings, even if they are unrelated to what you are reading. Those impressions may be the very things that your Heavenly Father wants you to learn.

Liken the Scriptures to Your Life

Consider how the stories and teachings you are reading apply to your life. For example, you could ask yourself, "What experiences have I had that are similar to what I am reading?" or "How can I follow the example of this person in the scriptures?"

Ask Questions as You Study

As you study the scriptures, questions may come to mind. These questions might relate to what you are reading or to your life in general. Ponder these questions and look for answers as you continue studying the scriptures.

Use Scripture Study Helps

To gain additional insights into the verses you read, use the footnotes, the Topical Guide, the Bible Dictionary, the Guide to the Scriptures (scriptures.ChurchofJesusChrist.org), and other study helps.

Consider the Context of the Scriptures

You can find meaningful insights about a scripture if you consider its context—the circumstances or setting of the scripture. For example, knowing the background and beliefs of the people a prophet spoke to can help you understand the intent of his words.

Record Your Thoughts and Feelings

There are various ways to record the impressions that come as you study. For example, you could mark a meaningful word or phrase and record your thoughts as a note in your scriptures. You could also keep a journal of the insights, feelings, and impressions you receive.

Study the Words of Latter-day Prophets and Apostles

Read what latter-day prophets and apostles have taught about the principles you find in the scriptures (for example, see conference.ChurchofJesusChrist.org and Church magazines).

Share Insights

Discussing insights from your personal study is not only a good way to teach others, but it also helps strengthen your understanding of what you have read.

Live by What You Learn

Scripture study should not only inspire us but also lead us to change the way we live. Listen to what the Spirit prompts you to do as you read, and then commit to act on those promptings.

Elder David A. Bednar said: "We should not expect the Church as an organization to teach or tell us everything we need to know and do to become devoted disciples and endure valiantly to the end [see Doctrine and Covenants 121:29]. Rather, our personal responsibility is to learn what we should learn, to live as we know we should live, and to become who the Master would have us become. And our homes are the ultimate setting for learning, living, and becoming" ("Prepared to Obtain Every Needful Thing," *Ensign* or *Liahona*, May 2019, 102).

Ideas to Improve Your Family Scripture Study

Regular family scripture study is a powerful way to help your family feel the influence of the Holy Ghost and learn the gospel. How much and how long you read as a family is not as important as being consistent in your efforts. As you make scripture study an important part of your family life, you will help your family members come closer to Heavenly Father and Jesus Christ and build their testimonies on the foundation of God's word. Consider counseling together about the following questions:

- How can your family members encourage each other to study the scriptures individually?

- What can your family members do to encourage each person to share what they are learning?

- How can you emphasize the principles you are learning in the New Testament in everyday teaching moments?

Remember that the home is the ideal place for gospel learning. You can learn and teach the gospel at home in ways that are not possible in a Church class. Be creative as you think of ways to help your family learn from the scriptures. Consider some of the following ideas to enhance your family scripture study.

Use Music

Sing songs that reinforce the principles taught in the scriptures. A suggested hymn or children's song is listed in each weekly outline. You might ask family members questions about words or phrases in the lyrics. In addition to singing, your family can perform actions that go with the songs or listen to the songs as background music while they are doing other activities. For more ideas, see "Including Sacred Music in Your Gospel Learning" in this resource.

Share Meaningful Scriptures

Give family members time to share scripture passages that they have found meaningful during their personal study.

Use Your Own Words

Invite family members to summarize in their own words what they learn from the scriptures you study.

Apply the Scriptures to Your Life

After reading a scripture passage, ask family members to share ways the passage applies to their lives.

Ask a Question

Invite family members to ask a gospel question, and then spend time looking for verses that can help answer the question.

Display a Scripture

Select a verse you find meaningful, and display it where family members will see it often. Invite other family members to take turns selecting a scripture to display.

Make a Scripture List

As a family, choose several verses that you would like to discuss during the coming week.

Memorize Scriptures

Select a scripture passage that is meaningful to your family, and invite family members to memorize it by repeating it daily or playing a memorization game.

Share Object Lessons

Find objects that relate to the gospel principles in the scripture passages you are reading as a family. Invite family members to talk about how each object relates to the teachings in the scriptures.

Pick a Topic

Let family members take turns choosing a topic that the family will study together. Use the Topical Guide, the Bible Dictionary, or the Guide to the Scriptures (scriptures.ChurchofJesusChrist.org) to find scripture passages about the topic.

Draw a Picture

Read a few verses as a family, and then allow time for family members to draw something that relates to what you read. Spend time discussing one another's drawings.

Act Out a Story

After reading a story, invite family members to act it out. Afterward, talk about how the story relates to the things that you are experiencing individually and as a family.

President Russell M. Nelson said: "I promise that as you diligently work to remodel your home into a center of gospel learning, over time *your* Sabbath days will truly be a delight. *Your* children will be excited to learn and to live the Savior's teachings, and the influence of the adversary in *your* life and in *your* home will decrease. Changes in your family will be dramatic and sustaining" ("Becoming Exemplary Latter-day Saints," *Ensign* or *Liahona*, Nov. 2018, 113).

Additional Resources

These resources can be found in the Gospel Library app and at ChurchofJesusChrist.org.

Hymns and *Children's Songbook*

Sacred music invites the Spirit, helps us feel the love of God, and teaches doctrine in a memorable way. In addition to using the print versions of *Hymns* and the *Children's Songbook*, you can find video and audio recordings of many hymns and children's songs at music.ChurchofJesusChrist.org and in the Sacred Music and Gospel Media apps.

Seminary and Institute Manuals

Seminary and institute manuals provide historical background and doctrinal commentary for principles and accounts found in the scriptures.

Church Magazines

The *Friend*, *For the Strength of Youth*, and the *Liahona* magazines provide stories and activities that can supplement the principles you are teaching from *Come, Follow Me—For Individuals and Families*.

Gospel Topics

In Gospel Topics (topics.ChurchofJesusChrist.org), you can find basic information about a variety of gospel topics, along with links to helpful resources, such as related general conference addresses, articles, scriptures, and videos. You can also find Gospel Topics Essays, which offer in-depth information about doctrinal and historical issues, as well as answers to a variety of questions about the Church and its teachings.

New Testament Stories

New Testament Stories can help children learn the doctrine and stories found in the New Testament. You can also find videos of these stories in the Gospel Library app and at GospelMedia.ChurchofJesusChrist.org.

Scripture Stories Coloring Book—New Testament

This resource contains fun coloring activity pages designed to enhance children's learning from the New Testament.

Videos and Art

Artwork, videos, and other media can help your family understand doctrine and visualize stories related to the scriptures. Visit Gospel Media at GospelMedia.ChurchofJesusChrist.org to browse the Church's collection of media resources. Gospel Media is also available as a mobile app. Many images that you can use are found in the *Gospel Art Book*.

Teaching in the Savior's Way

Teaching in the Savior's Way can help you learn about and apply principles of Christlike teaching.

Teaching Young Children

If you have young children in your family, here are some activities that can help them learn:

- *Sing.* Hymns and songs from the *Children's Songbook* teach doctrine powerfully. Use the topics index at the back of the *Children's Songbook* to find songs that relate to the gospel principles you are teaching. Help your children relate the messages of the songs to their lives. (See also "Including Sacred Music in Your Gospel Learning" in this resource.)

- *Listen to or act out a story.* Young children love stories—from the scriptures, from your life, from your family history, and from Church magazines. Look for ways to involve them in storytelling. They can hold pictures or objects, draw pictures of what they are hearing, act out the story, or even help tell the story. Help your children recognize the gospel truths in the stories you share.

- *Read a scripture.* Young children may not be able to read very much, but you can still engage them in learning from the scriptures. You may need to focus on a single verse, key phrase, or word. The children may even be able to memorize short phrases from the scriptures if they repeat them a few times. As they hear the word of God, they will feel the Spirit.

- *Look at a picture or watch a video.* When you show your children a picture or video related to a gospel principle or scripture story, ask them questions that help them learn from what they are seeing. For example, you could ask, "What is happening in this picture or video? How does it make you feel?" The Gospel Media app, GospelMedia.ChurchofJesusChrist. org, and children.ChurchofJesusChrist.org are good places to look for pictures and videos.

- *Create.* Children can build, draw, or color something related to the story or principle they are learning.

- *Participate in object lessons.* A simple object lesson can help your children understand a gospel principle that is difficult to comprehend. When using object lessons, find ways to let your children participate. They will learn more from an interactive experience than from just watching a demonstration.

- *Role-play.* When children role-play a situation they are likely to encounter in real life, they are better able to understand how a gospel principle applies to their lives.

- *Repeat activities.* Young children may need to hear concepts multiple times to understand them. Don't be afraid to repeat stories or activities often. For example, you might share a scripture story several times in different ways—by reading from the scriptures, summarizing in your own words, showing a video, letting your children help you tell the story, inviting them to act out the story, and so on.

Including Sacred Music in Your Gospel Learning

Singing Primary songs and hymns can bless you and your family in many ways. These ideas can help you use sacred music as you strive to learn and live the gospel.

- *Learn doctrinal principles.* Look for truths taught in the songs you sing or listen to. This may lead to gospel discussions about these truths throughout the day. Sing or listen to Primary songs or hymns that teach about Jesus Christ and His gospel. Pay attention to ways the Holy Ghost testifies of the Savior and His teachings.

- *Recognize music's power.* Singing or listening to Primary songs and hymns can be a blessing in times of need. For instance, singing a song could calm a child at bedtime, create joy as your family works together, uplift a neighbor who is sick, or comfort someone who feels anxious.

- *Share experiences.* Share personal and family experiences that relate to the messages of the songs. You can also share related scripture stories.

- *Involve your family.* Your family will learn more from songs if they are actively participating. To involve family members, you could invite an older child to help teach a song to younger siblings or invite children to teach the family a song they learned in Primary. You could also let family members take turns leading a song.

- *Be creative.* Use a variety of ways to learn sacred music as a family. For instance, you could do actions that go with words and phrases in a song. Or you could take turns acting out parts of a song while other family members try to guess the song. Your family might enjoy singing songs at different speeds or volumes. The Gospel Library app and the Gospel for Kids app have audio recordings and videos that can help you learn the songs. You could also make playlists of sacred music to listen to.

For more ideas, see the sections "Using Music to Teach Doctrine" and "Helping Children Learn and Remember Primary Songs and Hymns," found in "Instructions for Singing Time and the Children's Sacrament Meeting Presentation" in *Come, Follow Me—For Primary*.

We Are Responsible for Our Own Learning

The purpose of the scriptures is to help you come unto Christ and become more deeply converted to His gospel. *Come, Follow Me—For Individuals and Families* can help you understand the scriptures and find in them the spiritual strength you and your family need. Then, in your Church classes, you will have opportunities to share insights and encourage your fellow Saints in their efforts to follow Christ.

RECORD YOUR IMPRESSIONS

"What seek ye?" Jesus asked the disciples of John the Baptist (John 1:38). You might ask yourself the same question—for what you find in the New Testament this year will greatly depend on what you seek. "Seek, and ye shall find" is the Savior's promise (Matthew 7:7). So ask the questions that come to your mind as you study, and then seek diligently for answers. In the New Testament you will read about the powerful spiritual experiences of disciples of Jesus Christ. As a faithful disciple of the Savior, you can have your own powerful spiritual experiences as you accept the Savior's invitation, found throughout this sacred volume, "Come, follow me" (Luke 18:22).

Ideas for Personal Scripture Study

To truly learn from the Savior, I must accept His invitation, "Come, follow me."

The Savior's invitation, "Come, follow me," applies to all—whether we are new on the path of discipleship or have walked it all our lives. This was His invitation to a rich young man who was striving to keep the commandments (see Matthew 19:16–22; Luke 18:18–23). What the young man learned—and what we all must learn—is that being a disciple means giving our whole souls to Heavenly Father and Jesus Christ. We progress in our discipleship as we identify what we lack, make changes, and seek to more fully follow Them.

Learning from the Savior starts when we strive to understand what He taught. For example, how does your understanding of humility deepen as you explore the following?

- The Savior's teachings (see Matthew 18:1–5; Luke 18:9–14)
- An example from His life (see John 13:1–15)

However, learning is not complete until we live what the Savior taught. How can you be more humble?

If you want to learn more, try this activity with another gospel principle, such as love or forgiveness.

I am responsible for my own learning.

Elder David A. Bednar taught: "We should not expect the Church as an organization to teach or tell us everything we need to know and do to become devoted disciples and endure valiantly to the end. Rather, our personal responsibility is to learn what we should learn, to live as we know we should live, and to become who the Master would have us become. And our homes are the ultimate setting for learning, living, and becoming" ("Prepared to Obtain Every Needful Thing," *Ensign* or *Liahona*, May 2019, 102).

What does it mean to take responsibility for your own learning? Look for possible answers in Elder Bednar's statement and in the following scriptures: John 7:17; 1 Thessalonians 5:21; James 1:5–6, 22; 2:17; 1 Nephi 10:17–19; 2 Nephi 4:15; Alma 32:27; and Doctrine and Covenants 18:18; 58:26–28; 88:118. What do you feel inspired to do to be more active in learning the gospel?

I need to know the truth for myself.

Perhaps you know people who never seem to lose their faith, no matter what happens in their lives. They may remind you of the five wise virgins in the Savior's parable (see Matthew 25:1–13). What you may not see are their diligent efforts to strengthen their testimonies of the truth.

How do we gain and nurture our own testimonies? Write down your thoughts as you ponder the following scriptures: Luke 11:9–13; John 5:39; 7:14–17; Acts 17:10–12; 1 Corinthians 2:9–11; and Alma 5:45–46. (See also Gospel Topics, "Testimony," topics.ChurchofJesusChrist.org.)

Each of us must gain a testimony for ourselves.

What should I do when I have questions?

As you seek spiritual knowledge, questions will come to your mind. The following principles can help you address questions in ways that build faith and testimony:

- *Seek understanding from God.* God is the source of all truth, and He reveals truth through the Holy Ghost, the scriptures, and His prophets and apostles.

- *Act in faith.* If answers don't come right away, trust that the Lord will reveal answers when the time is right. In the meantime, keep living by the truth you already know.

- *Keep an eternal perspective.* Try to see things as the Lord sees them, not as the world does. View your questions in the context of our Heavenly Father's plan of salvation.

 Ideas for Family Scripture Study and Home Evening

Matthew 13:1–23. To help your family prepare to learn from the New Testament this year, you could read the parable of the sower. Your family might enjoy going outside and looking for the different types of ground described in the parable. How can we make our hearts like the "good ground" Jesus described? (Matthew 13:8).

Galatians 5:22–23; Philippians 4:8. President Russell M. Nelson has invited you to "transform [your] home into a sanctuary of faith" and to "remodel your home into a center of gospel learning." To those who do these things, he promised: "*Your* children will be excited to learn and to live the Savior's teachings, and the influence of the adversary in *your* life and in *your* home will decrease. Changes in your family will be dramatic and sustaining" ("Becoming Exemplary Latter-day Saints," *Ensign* or *Liahona*, Nov. 2018, 113).

The beginning of the new year is a good time to hold a family council about making your home "a sanctuary of faith" and "a center of gospel learning." What ideas about how to do this come to mind as we read Galatians 5:22–23 and Philippians 4:8? Maybe your family could set personal and family goals to study the New Testament this coming year. What can we do to remind ourselves of our goals?

For more ideas for teaching children, see this week's outline in *Come, Follow Me—For Primary*.

Suggested song: "Teach Me to Walk in the Light," *Children's Songbook*, 177.

Improving Personal Study

Look for doctrine. A doctrine is an eternal, unchanging truth. President Boyd K. Packer declared that "true doctrine, understood, changes attitudes and behavior" ("Little Children," *Ensign*, Nov. 1986, 17). As you and your family study the scriptures, look for truths that can help you to live more like the Savior.

Light of the World, by Brent Borup

Matthew 1; Luke 1

"BE IT UNTO ME ACCORDING TO THY WORD"

As you read and ponder Matthew 1 and Luke 1, record the spiritual impressions you receive. What doctrinal truths do you find? What messages will be of most value to you and your family? The study ideas in this outline may help you discover additional insights.

RECORD YOUR IMPRESSIONS

From a mortal perspective, it was impossible. A virgin could not conceive—nor could a barren woman who was well past childbearing years. But God had a plan for the birth of His Son and the birth of John the Baptist, so both Mary and Elisabeth, against all earthly odds, became mothers. It can be helpful to remember their miraculous experiences whenever we face something that seems impossible. Can we overcome our weaknesses? Can we touch the heart of an unresponsive family member? Gabriel could easily have been speaking to us when he reminded Mary, "With God nothing shall be impossible" (Luke 1:37). And Mary's response can also be ours when God reveals His will: "Be it unto me according to thy word" (Luke 1:38).

 Ideas for Personal Scripture Study

Who were Matthew and Luke?

Matthew was a Jewish publican, or tax collector, whom Jesus called as one of His Apostles (see Matthew 10:3; see also Bible Dictionary, "Publicans"). Matthew wrote his Gospel mainly to fellow Jews; therefore, he chose to emphasize Old Testament prophecies about the Messiah that were fulfilled through Jesus's life and ministry.

Luke was a Gentile (non-Jewish) physician who traveled with the Apostle Paul. He wrote his Gospel after the Savior's death primarily to a non-Jewish audience. He testified of Jesus Christ as the Savior of both the Gentiles and the Jews. He recorded eyewitness accounts of events in the Savior's life, and he included more stories involving women compared to the other Gospels.

See also Bible Dictionary, "Gospels," "Matthew," "Luke."

MATTHEW 1:18–25; LUKE 1:26–35

Jesus Christ was born of a mortal mother and an immortal Father.

In Matthew 1:18–25 and Luke 1:26–35, notice how Matthew and Luke described the miracle of Jesus's birth. How do their descriptions strengthen your faith in the Savior? Why is it important to you to know that Jesus was both the Son of God and the son of Mary?

President Russell M. Nelson explained that the Atonement of Jesus Christ "required a personal sacrifice by an immortal being not subject to death. Yet He must die and take up His own body again. The Savior was the only one who could accomplish this. From His mother He inherited power to die. From His Father He obtained power over death" ("Constancy amid Change," *Ensign*, Nov. 1993, 34).

LUKE 1:5–25, 57–80

God's blessings come in His own time.

If you find yourself having to wait for a blessing or if it seems that God isn't hearing your prayers, the story of Elisabeth and Zacharias can be a reminder that He hasn't forgotten you. As Elder Jeffrey R. Holland promised: "While we work and wait together for the answers to some of our prayers, I offer you my apostolic promise that they are heard and they are answered, though perhaps not at the time or in the way we wanted. But they are *always* answered at the time and in the way an omniscient and eternally compassionate parent should answer them" ("Waiting on the Lord," *Ensign* or *Liahona*, Nov. 2020, 115–16). How did Zacharias and Elisabeth remain faithful? (see Luke 1:5–25, 57–80). Do you find yourself waiting for a blessing? What do you feel the Lord expects of you while you wait?

MATTHEW 1:18–25; LUKE 1:26–38

After faithfully waiting, Elisabeth and Zacharias were blessed with a son.

The faithful willingly submit to God's will.

Like Mary, we sometimes find that God's plans for our life are quite different from what we had planned. What do you learn from Mary about accepting God's will? In the following tables, write statements from the angel and Mary (see Luke 1:26–38), along with the messages that you find in their statements:

The angel's words to Mary	Message for me
"The Lord is with thee" (verse 28).	The Lord is aware of my situation and struggles.

Mary's reactions	Message for me
"How shall this be?" (verse 34).	It's OK to ask questions to better understand God's will.

As you read about Joseph's righteous example in Matthew 1:18–25, what do you learn about accepting God's will? What additional insights do you learn from the experiences of Zacharias and Elisabeth? (see Luke 1).

See also Luke 22:42; Bible Dictionary, "Gabriel."

LUKE 1:46–55

Mary testified of Jesus Christ's mission.

Mary's words in Luke 1:46–55 foretold aspects of the Savior's mission. What do you learn about Jesus Christ from Mary's statements? You might compare these verses with Hannah's words in 1 Samuel 2:1–10 and with Jesus's Beatitudes in Matthew 5:3–12. What does the Spirit teach you as you ponder these verses?

 Ideas for Family Scripture Study and Home Evening

Matthew 1:1–17. As your family reads the genealogy of Jesus, you might discuss your own family history and share some stories about your ancestors. How does knowing about your family history bless your family? For more family history activities, see FamilySearch.org/discovery.

Matthew 1:20; Luke 1:11–13, 30. Why might the people in these verses have been fearful? What causes us to feel fearful? How does God invite us to "fear not"?

Luke 1:37. To help your family build faith that "with God nothing shall be impossible," you could search Luke 1 together and find things God did that might be considered impossible. What other stories can we share—from the scriptures or our own lives—in which God did seemingly impossible things? Searching through the *Gospel Art Book* could provide ideas.

Luke 1:46–55. What are some of the "great things" the Savior has done for us? What could it mean for our souls to "magnify the Lord"?

For more ideas for teaching children, see this week's outline in *Come, Follow Me—For Primary*.

Suggested song: "He Sent His Son," *Children's Songbook*, 34–35.

Improving Our Teaching

Apply the scriptures to your life. After reading a scripture passage, invite family members to apply it to their lives (see *Teaching in the Savior's Way*, 21). For instance, how can family members apply what they learn from Matthew 1 and Luke 1 about responding to the Lord's call?

Blessed Art Thou among Women, by Walter Rane

Matthew 2; Luke 2

WE HAVE COME TO WORSHIP HIM

As you read Matthew 2 and Luke 2, pay attention to any spiritual insights you receive. The study ideas in this outline can help you identify important and relevant principles in these chapters.

RECORD YOUR IMPRESSIONS

From the day of His birth, it was clear that Jesus was no ordinary child. It wasn't just the new star in the heavens or the joyous angelic proclamation that made Jesus's infancy remarkable. It was also the fact that such a variety of faithful people—from different nations, professions, and backgrounds—felt immediately drawn to Him. Even before He uttered His invitation to "come, follow me," they came (Luke 18:22). Not everyone came to Him, of course. There were many who paid Him no notice, and a jealous ruler even sought His life. But the humble, pure, devoted seekers of righteousness saw Him for who He was—their promised Messiah. Their devotion inspires our own, for the "good tidings of great joy" brought to the shepherds were for "all people," and the "Saviour, which is Christ the Lord" was born that day unto all of us (see Luke 2:10–11).

 Ideas for Personal Scripture Study

Jesus Christ was born in humble circumstances.

Although Jesus Christ had glory with God the Father "before the world was" (John 17:5), He was willing to be born in lowly circumstances and live among us on earth. As you read Luke 2:1–7, ponder what this account of His birth teaches you about Him. Try to identify details or insights in this story that you hadn't noticed before. How does noticing these things affect your feelings toward Him?

See also "The Christ Child" (video), ChurchofJesusChrist.org.

MATTHEW 2:1–12; LUKE 2:8–38

There are many witnesses of the birth of Christ.

The birth and infancy of Christ were marked by witnesses and worshippers from many walks of life. As you explore their stories, what do you learn about ways to worship and witness of Christ?

Witness of Christ	What do I learn about worshipping and witnessing of Christ?
Shepherds (Luke 2:8–20)	
Simeon (Luke 2:25–35)	
Anna (Luke 2:36–38)	
Wise Men (Matthew 2:1–12)	

See also 1 Nephi 11:13–23; 3 Nephi 1:5–21; "Shepherds Learn of the Birth of Christ" and "The Christ Child Is Presented at the Temple" (videos), ChurchofJesusChrist.org.

MATTHEW 2:13–23

Parents can receive revelation to protect their families.

Joseph never could have done what he was asked to do—protect Jesus in His childhood—without heaven's help. Like the Wise Men, he received a revelation that warned him of danger. As you read about Joseph's experience in Matthew 2:13–23, think about physical and spiritual dangers that face us today. Ponder experiences when you have felt God's guidance in protecting you and your loved ones. Consider sharing these experiences with others. What can you do to receive such guidance in the future?

Additionally, you might consider watching the video "The First Christmas Spirit" (ChurchofJesusChrist.org) for a depiction of what Joseph may have felt as he faced the responsibility of caring for the Son of God.

LUKE 2:40–52

Even as a youth, Jesus was focused on doing His Father's will.

As a young man, the Savior taught the gospel so powerfully that even the teachers in the temple were astonished at His "understanding and answers" (Luke 2:47). What do you learn from these verses about the Savior as a young man? How are young people you know trying to "be about [their] Father's business"? (Luke 2:49). How have youth and children helped you gain a deeper understanding of the gospel? What else do you learn from the example of Jesus's childhood in Luke 2:40–52 and in Joseph Smith Translation, Matthew 3:24–26 (in the Bible appendix)?

"Wist ye not that I must be about my Father's business?" (Luke 2:49).

What is the Joseph Smith Translation?

Because "many plain and precious" truths were lost from the Bible over the centuries (1 Nephi 13:28; see also Moses 1:41), the Lord commanded Joseph Smith to make an inspired revision of the Bible, known as the Joseph Smith Translation. Many revisions made by the Prophet are included in the appendix of the Latter-day Saint edition of the scriptures. The Latter-day Saint edition of the King James Version of the Bible also contains footnotes with the Prophet's revisions. Joseph Smith's translation of Matthew 24, known as Joseph Smith—Matthew, can be found in the Pearl of Great Price. For more information, see "Joseph Smith Translation (JST)" in the Bible Dictionary and the Gospel Topics article "Bible, Inerrancy of" (topics .ChurchofJesusChrist.org).

 Ideas for Family Scripture Study and Home Evening

Luke 2. Invite family members to select a person described in Luke 2, read a few verses about that person's interactions with the Savior, and share something that they learned that increases their faith in Jesus Christ. Sing together "Mary's Lullaby" or "The Nativity Song" (*Children's Songbook*, 44–45, 52–53). What do we learn from these songs about the Savior's birth?

Consider how artwork might enhance your discussion about Christ's birth. (For examples, see *Gospel Art Book* or history.ChurchofJesusChrist.org/exhibit/birth-of-Christ.)

Matthew 2:1–12. What do we learn about seeking and finding the Savior from the example of the Wise Men?

Luke 2:41–49. What is the "Father's business"? (Luke 2:49; see Moses 1:39; *General Handbook: Serving in The Church of Jesus Christ of Latter-day Saints*, 1.2, ChurchofJesusChrist.org). What do we learn about that business from the story in Luke 2:41–49? Consider writing down some ways your family can participate in the Father's business and placing them in a jar. During the coming week, as your family looks for ways to help with Heavenly Father's work, they can select ideas from the jar. Plan a time when you will share your experiences.

Luke 2:52. What can we learn from Luke 2:52 about how Jesus developed in His life? What personal or family goals can we set to increase "in wisdom and stature, and in favour with God and man"?

For more ideas for teaching children, see this week's outline in *Come, Follow Me—For Primary*.

Suggested song: "Stars Were Gleaming," *Children's Songbook*, 37.

Improving Personal Study

Use scripture study helps. To gain additional insights as you study the scriptures, use resources like the footnotes, Topical Guide, Bible Dictionary, Guide to the Scriptures, and other study helps found at ChurchofJesusChrist.org.

The Savior of the World came to earth in humble circumstances.

John 1

WE HAVE FOUND THE MESSIAH

As you read and ponder John 1, record the impressions you receive. What messages do you find that will be of most value to you and your family? What could you share in your Church classes?

RECORD YOUR IMPRESSIONS

Have you ever wondered whether you would have recognized Jesus of Nazareth as the Son of God if you had been alive during His mortal ministry? For years, faithful Israelites, including Andrew, Peter, Philip, and Nathanael, had waited and prayed for the coming of the promised Messiah. When they met Him, how did they know that He was the One they had been seeking? The same way all of us come to know the Savior—by accepting the invitation to "come and see" for ourselves (John 1:39). We read about Him in the scriptures. We hear His doctrine. We observe His way of living. We feel His Spirit. Along the way, we discover, as Nathanael did, that the Savior knows us and loves us and wants to prepare us to receive "greater things" (John 1:50).

 Ideas for Personal Scripture Study

Who was John?

John was a disciple of John the Baptist and later became one of the first followers of Jesus Christ and one of His Twelve Apostles. He wrote the Gospel of John, several epistles, and the book of Revelation. In his Gospel, he referred to himself as the disciple "whom Jesus loved" and the "other disciple" (John 13:23; 20:3). John's zeal for preaching the gospel was so strong that he asked to stay on the earth until the Savior's Second Coming so he could bring souls unto Christ (see Doctrine and Covenants 7:1–6).

See also Bible Dictionary, "John," "John, Gospel of."

JOHN 1:1–5

Jesus Christ was "in the beginning with God."

John began his Gospel by describing the work that Christ performed before He was born: "In the beginning . . . the Word [Jesus Christ] was with God." What do you learn from verses 1–5 about the Savior and His work? You can find helpful clarifications in Joseph Smith Translation, John 1:1–5 (in the Bible appendix). As you begin your study of the Savior's life, why is it important to know about His premortal work?

See also Gospel Topics, "Jesus Christ Chosen as Savior," topics.ChurchofJesusChrist.org.

JOHN 1:1–18

Jesus Christ is the "true Light," the Son of God.

John was inspired to seek the Savior because of the testimony of John the Baptist, who declared that he "was sent to bear witness of . . . the true Light" (John 1:8–9). John himself also bore powerful witness of the life and mission of the Savior.

It might be interesting to make a list of truths that John included in his opening testimony of Christ (verses 1–18; see also Joseph Smith Translation, John 1:1–19 [in the Bible appendix]). Why do you think that John began his Gospel with these truths? Consider writing your witness of Jesus Christ—what would you want to share? What experiences have helped you come to know and follow the Savior? Who might be blessed by hearing your testimony?

JOHN 1:11–13

Jesus Christ gives us "power to become" the sons and daughters of God.

Although we are all spirit daughters and sons of God the Father, when we sin we become estranged, or separated, from Him. Jesus Christ offers us a way back through His atoning sacrifice. Ponder what John 1:11–13 teaches about becoming daughters and sons of God. Consider also what these scriptures teach about how we receive this gift: Romans 8:14–18; Mosiah 5:7–9; Doctrine and Covenants 25:1. What does it mean to you to have "power to become" a daughter or son of God?

JOHN 1:18

The Father bears record of His Son.

John 1:18 states that no one has seen God. However, the Joseph Smith Translation of this verse clarifies that "no man hath seen God at any time, except he hath borne record of the Son" (see John 1:18, footnote *c*). Consider reviewing the following instances in which God the Father was heard bearing record of the Son: Matthew 3:17; 17:5; 3 Nephi 11:6–7; Joseph Smith—History 1:17.

Why is it a blessing to have these accounts? What do they teach you about Jesus Christ's relationship with His Father?

 ## Ideas for Family Scripture Study and Home Evening

As we study the scriptures, we will receive inspiration for our lives.

John 1:4–10. How might you help your family visualize what they read about light in these verses? You could let family members take turns shining a light in a dark room and sharing how the Savior is the Light of their lives. Then, as you read John 1:4–10, family members might have additional insight into John's testimony of Jesus Christ, the Light of the World.

John 1:35–36. Why might John the Baptist have called Jesus "the Lamb of God"? What do we learn about this title from Elder Jeffrey R. Holland's message "Behold the Lamb of God" or Elder Gerrit W. Gong's message "Good Shepherd, Lamb of God"? (*Ensign* or *Liahona*, May 2019, 44–46, 97–101)

John 1:35–46. What were the results of John's testimony? What can your family learn from the people described in these verses about how to share the gospel? See also the video "Inviting Others to 'Come and See'" (ChurchofJesusChrist.org).

John 1:45–51. What did Nathanael do that helped him gain a testimony of the Savior? Invite family members to talk about how they have gained their testimonies.

For more ideas for teaching children, see this week's outline in *Come, Follow Me—For Primary*.

Suggested hymn: "The Lord Is My Light," *Hymns*, no. 89.

Improving Our Teaching

Share object lessons. Invite family members to find objects that they can use to help them understand principles found in the scriptures you are reading as a family. For instance, they might use a candle to represent the Light of Christ (see John 1:4).

Jehovah Creates the Earth, by Walter Rane

Matthew 3; Mark 1; Luke 3

"PREPARE YE THE WAY OF THE LORD"

Begin by reading Matthew 3; Mark 1; and Luke 3. As you pray for the Holy Ghost to help you understand these chapters, He will give you insights that are especially for you. Record these impressions, and make plans to act on them.

RECORD YOUR IMPRESSIONS

Jesus Christ and His gospel can change you. Luke quoted an ancient prophecy of Isaiah that described the effect that the Savior's coming would have: "Every valley shall be filled, and every mountain and hill shall be brought low; and the crooked shall be made straight, and the rough ways shall be made smooth" (Luke 3:5; see also Isaiah 40:4). This is a message for all of us, including those who think they cannot change. If something as permanent as a mountain can be flattened, then surely the Lord can help us straighten our own crooked paths (see Luke 3:4–5). As we accept John the Baptist's invitation to repent and change, we prepare our minds and hearts to receive Jesus Christ so that we too can "see the salvation of God" (Luke 3:6).

 Ideas for Personal Scripture Study

Who was Mark?

Among the authors of the Gospels, we know the least about Mark. We know that he was a missionary companion of Paul, Peter, and several other missionaries. Many biblical scholars believe that Peter directed Mark to record the events of the Savior's life. Mark's Gospel was likely written before the other three.

See also Bible Dictionary, "Mark."

Repentance is a mighty change of mind and heart.

The mission of John the Baptist was to prepare the hearts of the people to receive the Savior and become more like Him. How did he do it? He proclaimed, "Repent ye" (Matthew 3:2). And he used images such as fruit and wheat to teach about repentance (see Luke 3:9, 17).

What other images do you find in the accounts of John the Baptist's ministry? (see Matthew 3:1–12; Mark 1:1–8; Luke 3:2–18). Consider marking them in your scriptures or drawing pictures of them. What do these images teach about the doctrine and necessity of repentance?

True repentance is "a change of mind, a fresh view about God, about oneself, and about the world. . . . [It means] a turning of the heart and will to God" (Bible Dictionary, "Repentance"). In Luke 3:7–14, what changes did John invite the people to make to prepare to receive Christ? How might this counsel apply to you? How can you show that you have truly repented? (see Luke 3:8).

See also Russell M. Nelson, "We Can Do Better and Be Better," *Ensign* or *Liahona*, May 2019, 67–69; Dallin H. Oaks, "Cleansed by Repentance," *Ensign* or *Liahona*, May 2019, 91–94.

Who were the Pharisees and Sadducees?

The Pharisees were members of a Jewish religious party who prided themselves on strict observance of the law of Moses and its rituals. The Sadducees were a wealthy Jewish class with great religious and political influence; they did not believe in the doctrine of resurrection. Both groups had strayed from the original intent of God's laws.

See also Matthew 23:23–28; Bible Dictionary, "Pharisees," "Sadducees."

Jesus Christ was baptized to "fulfil all righteousness."

When you were baptized, you followed the example of the Savior. Compare what you learn from the accounts of the Savior's baptism with what happened during your baptism.

The Savior's Baptism	My Baptism
Who baptized Jesus, and what authority did he hold?	Who baptized you, and what authority did he hold?
Where was Jesus baptized?	Where were you baptized?
How was Jesus baptized?	How were you baptized?
Why was Jesus baptized?	Why were you baptized?
How did Heavenly Father show that He was pleased with Jesus?	How did Heavenly Father show that He was pleased when you were baptized? How has He shown His approval since then?

See also 2 Nephi 31; Mosiah 18:8–11; Doctrine and Covenants 20:37, 68–74; "The Baptism of Jesus" (video), ChurchofJesusChrist.org.

The members of the Godhead are three separate beings.

The Bible contains numerous evidences that the members of the Godhead are three separate beings. The accounts of the Savior's baptism are one example. As you read these accounts, ponder what you learn about the Godhead. Why are these doctrines important to you?

See also Genesis 1:26; Matthew 17:1–5; John 17:1–3; Acts 7:55–56; Doctrine and Covenants 130:22.

Ideas for Family Scripture Study and Home Evening

Matthew 3. John the Baptist held the Aaronic Priesthood. What can we learn from John's example about the purposes of the Aaronic Priesthood? What blessings do we receive because of the Aaronic Priesthood? If you have a young man in your family, you might take time to help him understand how he can use the Aaronic Priesthood to bless others. (See also Doctrine and Covenants 13:1; 20:46–60.)

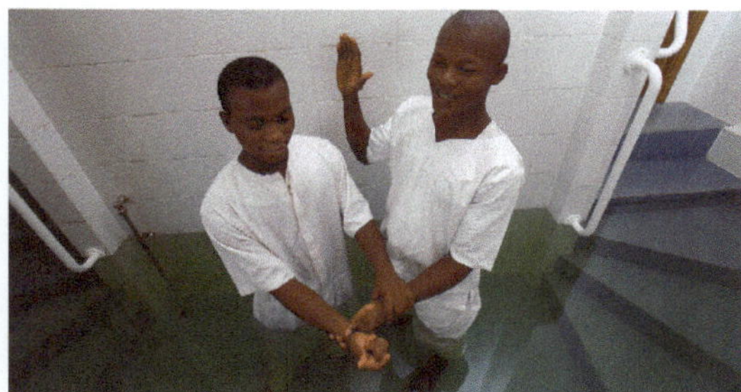

When we are baptized, our sins are washed away.

Matthew 3:11–17; Mark 1:9–11; Luke 3:21–22. Have members of your family seen someone be baptized or confirmed a member of the Church? What did family members feel? Perhaps you could teach them about the symbolism of baptism and confirmation. How is being baptized and confirmed like a new birth? Why are we fully immersed in water when we are baptized? Why do we wear white when we are baptized? Why is the gift of the Holy Ghost described as a "baptism of fire"? (Doctrine and Covenants 20:41; see also Bible Dictionary, "Baptism," "Holy Ghost").

Matthew 3:17; Mark 1:11; Luke 3:22. When have we felt that God has been pleased with us? What can we do as a family to please God?

For more ideas for teaching children, see this week's outline in *Come, Follow Me—For Primary*.

Suggested song: "Baptism," *Children's Songbook*, 100–101.

Improving Personal Study

Ask the Lord for help. The scriptures were given by revelation, and to truly understand them we need personal revelation. The Lord has promised, "Ask, and it shall be given you; seek, and ye shall find; knock, and it shall be opened unto you" (Matthew 7:7).

John the Baptist Baptizing Jesus, by Greg K. Olsen

Matthew 4; Luke 4–5

"THE SPIRIT OF THE LORD IS UPON ME"

The Savior used the scriptures both to resist Satan's temptations and to testify of His own divine mission (see Luke 4:1–21). Ponder how the scriptures can build your faith and your resolve to resist temptation.

RECORD YOUR IMPRESSIONS

From His youth, Jesus seemed to be aware that He had a unique, sacred mission. But as Jesus prepared to begin His earthly ministry, the adversary sought to plant doubt in the Savior's mind. "*If* thou be the Son of God," Satan said (Luke 4:3, italics added). But the Savior had communed with His Father in Heaven. He knew the scriptures, and He knew who He was. To Him, Satan's offer—"All this power will I give thee" (Luke 4:6)—was a hollow one, for the Savior's lifelong preparation allowed Him to receive "the power of the Spirit" (Luke 4:14). So despite temptation, trials, and rejection, Jesus Christ never wavered from His appointed work: "I must preach the kingdom of God . . . for therefore am I sent" (Luke 4:43).

 Ideas for Personal Scripture Study

MATTHEW 4:1–2

Communing with God prepares me to serve Him.

To prepare for His mission, Jesus went into the wilderness "to be with God" (Joseph Smith Translation, Matthew 4:1 [in Matthew 4:1, footnote *b*]). Think of what you do to feel close to God. How does this prepare you for the work He wants you to do?

Jesus Christ set the example for me by resisting temptation.

Sometimes people feel guilty when they are tempted to sin. But even the Savior, who lived "without sin" (Hebrews 4:15), was tempted. Jesus Christ knows the temptations we face and how to help us overcome them (see Hebrews 2:18; Alma 7:11–12).

As you read Matthew 4:1–11 and Luke 4:1–13, what do you learn that can help you when you face temptations? You could organize your thoughts in a table like this one:

Jesus Christ	Me
What did Satan tempt Christ to do?	What does Satan tempt me to do?
How did Christ prepare to resist temptation?	How can I prepare to resist temptation?

What additional insights do you gain from the Joseph Smith Translation of Matthew 4? (see footnotes throughout Matthew 4).

See also 1 Corinthians 10:13; Alma 13:28; Moses 1:10–22; Gospel Topics, "Temptation," topics.ChurchofJesusChrist.org.

Jesus Christ is the prophesied Messiah.

If you were asked to describe what Jesus Christ was sent to earth to do, what would you say? By quoting one of Isaiah's prophecies about the Messiah, the Savior described aspects of His own mission (see Luke 4:18–19; Isaiah 61:1–2). What do you learn about His mission as you read these verses?

What are some ways the Savior invites you to participate in His work?

Although the Jews had been waiting for centuries for Isaiah's prophecy to be fulfilled, many did not accept that Jesus was the Messiah when He declared, "This day is this scripture fulfilled in your ears" (Luke 4:21). As you read Luke 4:20–30 (see also Mark 6:1–6), try to put yourself in the place of the people of Nazareth. Is there anything that might prevent you from fully accepting Christ as your personal Savior?

See also Mosiah 3:5–12; "Jesus Declares He Is the Messiah" (video), ChurchofJesusChrist.org.

As I trust in the Lord, He can help me reach my divine potential.

President Ezra Taft Benson taught, "Men and women who turn their lives over to God will discover that He can make a lot more out of their lives than they can" (*Teachings of Presidents of the Church: Ezra Taft Benson* [2014], 42). Note how this happened to Simon Peter and his fellow fishermen. Jesus saw something greater in them than they saw in themselves. He wanted to make them "fishers of men" (Matthew 4:19; see also Luke 5:10).

As you read Matthew 4:18–22 and Luke 5:1–11, ponder what Jesus Christ is helping you to become. How have you felt Him inviting you to follow Him? How can you show the Lord that you are willing to forsake all things to follow Him? (see Luke 5:11).

 ## Ideas for Family Scripture Study and Home Evening

Matthew 4:1–2; Luke 4:1–2. What insights can we gain from this account about the power of fasting? To help your family learn about fasting, you might use "Fasting and Fast Offerings" in Gospel Topics (topics.ChurchofJesusChrist.org). Family members could share experiences they have had with fasting. Perhaps you could prayerfully make plans to fast together for a specific purpose.

Matthew 4:3–4; Luke 4:3–4. When Satan tempted Christ to turn a stone to bread, he challenged Christ's divine identity by saying, "*If* thou be the Son of God" (Matthew 4:3, italics added). Why does Satan try to make us doubt our divine identity—and the Savior's? How does he try to do this? (See also Moses 1:10–23.)

Joseph Smith Translation, Matthew 4:11. After Jesus was physically and spiritually tested, His thoughts turned to the needs of John the Baptist, who was in prison: "And now Jesus knew that John was cast into prison, and he sent angels, and, behold, they came and ministered unto him [John]" (Joseph Smith Translation, Matthew 4:11 [in Matthew 4:11, footnote *a*]). How are we blessed as we follow Christ's example of thinking of others?

Luke 4:16–21. Do we know anyone who is brokenhearted or who needs to be "set at liberty"? (Luke 4:18). How can we help others receive the Savior's healing and deliverance? You might also discuss how performing temple ordinances helps bring "deliverance to the captives" (Luke 4:18).

For more ideas for teaching children, see this week's outline in *Come, Follow Me—For Primary.*

Suggested hymn: "Come, Follow Me," *Hymns,* no. 116.

Improving Our Teaching

Live the gospel of Jesus Christ. "Perhaps the most important thing you can do [as a parent or teacher] is to . . . live the gospel with all your heart. . . . This is the principal way to qualify for the companionship of the Holy Ghost. You don't have to be perfect, just diligently trying—and seeking forgiveness through the Savior's Atonement whenever you stumble" (*Teaching in the Savior's Way,* 13).

Christ Calling the Apostles James and John, Edward Armitage (1817–96)/Sheffield Galleries and Museums Trust, UK/© Museums Sheffield/The Bridgeman Art Library International

John 2–4

"YE MUST BE BORN AGAIN"

As you read John 2–4, the Spirit will teach you things about your own conversion. Make note of His promptings. You may find additional spiritual insights from the study ideas in this outline.

RECORD YOUR IMPRESSIONS

At a marriage feast in Cana, Christ changed water into wine—an event John called the "beginning of miracles" (John 2:11). That's true in more than one sense. While this was the first miracle Jesus performed publicly, it can also symbolize another miraculous beginning—the process of our hearts being transformed as we become ever more like our Savior. This miracle of a lifetime begins with the decision to follow Jesus Christ, to change and live a better life through Him. This miracle can be so life-changing that being "born again" is one of the best ways to describe it (John 3:7). But rebirth is just the beginning of the path of discipleship. Christ's words to the Samaritan woman at the well remind us that if we continue on this path, eventually the gospel will become "a well of water" inside us, "springing up into everlasting life" (John 4:14).

 Ideas for Personal Scripture Study

JOHN 2:1–11

Jesus Christ's miracles "manifested forth his glory."

As you read about the Savior changing water into wine in John 2:1–11, you may gain additional insights by considering the perspectives of the different people who were there, including Mary, the disciples, and others. If you had witnessed the events described here, what would your impressions of Jesus have been? What does this miracle teach you about Him?

JOHN 3:1–21

I must be born again to enter the kingdom of God.

When Nicodemus came to Jesus in private, he was a cautious observer. Later, however, he publicly defended Jesus (see John 7:45–52) and joined the believers at the Savior's burial (see John 19:38–40). What teachings do you find in John 3:1–21 that might have inspired Nicodemus to follow Jesus and be born again?

The Prophet Joseph Smith taught, "Being born again, comes by the Spirit of God through ordinances" (*Teachings of Presidents of the Church: Joseph Smith* [2007], 95). What role did your baptism and confirmation—being "born of water and of the Spirit" (John 3:5)—play in your being born again? What are you doing to continue this process of change? (see Alma 5:11–14).

See also Mosiah 5:7; 27:25–26; David A. Bednar, "Ye Must Be Born Again," *Ensign* or *Liahona*, May 2007, 19–22.

JOHN 3:16–17

Heavenly Father shows His love for me through Jesus Christ.

Elder Jeffrey R. Holland taught, "The first great *truth* of all eternity is that God loves *us* with all of *His* heart, might, mind, and strength" ("Tomorrow the Lord Will Do Wonders among You," *Ensign* or *Liahona*, May 2016, 127). How have you felt the love of God through the gift of His Son?

The sacrament provides a time to reflect on the love of God and the gift of His Son. What sacrament hymns help you feel this love? What could you do to make the sacrament more meaningful?

As you continue to read about the Savior's teachings and ministry, ask yourself how the things you read help you understand and feel God's love.

JOHN 4:24

Is God a spirit?

Some may be confused by Jesus's statement that God is a spirit. The Joseph Smith Translation of this verse provides an important clarification: "For unto such hath God promised his Spirit" (in John 4:24, footnote *a*). Modern revelation also teaches that God has a body of flesh and bones (see Doctrine and Covenants 130:22–23; see also Genesis 5:1–3; Hebrews 1:1–3).

JOHN 4:5–26

Christ offers me His living water.

What might Jesus have meant when He told the Samaritan woman that whoever drinks the water He offers will never thirst? How is the gospel like living water?

Christ's gospel is the living water that nourishes our souls.

One of the Savior's messages to the Samaritan woman was that how we worship is more important than where we worship (see John 4:21–24). What are you doing to "worship the Father in spirit and in truth"? (John 4:23).

See also Guide to the Scriptures, "Worship," scriptures.ChurchofJesusChrist.org; Dean M. Davies, "The Blessings of Worship," *Ensign* or *Liahona*, Nov. 2016, 93–95.

Ideas for Family Scripture Study and Home Evening

John 2–4. As your family reads these chapters this week, pay special attention to how the Savior used everyday things—birth, wind, water, and food—to teach spiritual truths. What items in your home can you use to teach spiritual truths?

As you study these chapters, consider watching videos together that depict these events: "Jesus Turns Water into Wine," "Jesus Cleanses the Temple," "Jesus Teaches of Being Born Again," and "Jesus Teaches a Samaritan Woman" (ChurchofJesusChrist.org).

John 2:13–17. What impure influences does your family need to keep out of your home so it will be a sacred place—like the temple? What will you do to keep those things out?

John 3:1–6. Talk with your family about the miracle of pregnancy and birth—the process of creating a living, intelligent being. Jesus taught that we must be reborn before entering the kingdom of God. Why is rebirth a good metaphor for the change required of us before we can enter the kingdom of God? How can we experience the process of spiritual rebirth?

John 3:16–17. Invite family members to restate these verses in their own words as if they were explaining them to a friend. How has Jesus Christ helped us feel God's love?

John 4:5–15. What was the Savior teaching us when He compared His gospel to living water? Maybe your family could look at some running water and describe the qualities of water. Why do we need to drink water every day? In what ways is Jesus Christ's gospel like "a well of water springing up into everlasting life"? (John 4:14).

For more ideas for teaching children, see this week's outline in *Come, Follow Me—For Primary.*

Suggested song: "God's Love," *Children's Songbook,* 97.

Improving Personal Study

Look for symbols. The scriptures often use objects, events, or actions to represent spiritual truths. These symbols can enrich your understanding of the doctrine being taught. For example, the Savior likened conversion to rebirth.

Living Water, by Simon Dewey

Matthew 5; Luke 6

"BLESSED ARE YE"

Pay attention to impressions you receive as you read Matthew 5 and Luke 6, and record them in a study journal or in some other way. This outline can help you identify some important principles in these chapters, but be open to others you discover in your study.

RECORD YOUR IMPRESSIONS

By this point in His ministry, it was clear that Jesus's teachings would be unlike what the people of His time were used to hearing. The poor will receive the kingdom of God? The meek will inherit the earth? Blessed are the persecuted? The scribes and Pharisees were not teaching such things. And yet those who truly understood God's law recognized truth in the Savior's words. "An eye for an eye" and "hate thine enemy" were lesser laws (Matthew 5:38, 43). But Jesus Christ had come to teach a higher law (see 3 Nephi 15:2–10), designed to help us one day become "perfect, even as [our] Father which is in heaven is perfect" (Matthew 5:48).

 Ideas for Personal Scripture Study

MATTHEW 5:1–12; LUKE 6:20–26, 46–49

Lasting happiness comes from living the way Jesus Christ taught.

Everybody wants to be happy, but not everyone looks for happiness in the same places. Some search for it in worldly power and position, others in wealth or in satisfying physical appetites. Jesus Christ came to teach the way to lasting happiness, to teach what it truly means to be blessed. What do you learn about obtaining lasting happiness from Matthew 5:1–12 and Luke 6:20–26? How is this different from the world's view of happiness?

What do these verses, together with Luke 6:46–49, teach you about being a disciple of Jesus Christ? What do you feel inspired to do to develop the qualities described in these verses?

See also Guide to the Scriptures, "Beatitudes," scriptures.ChurchofJesusChrist.org; "Sermon on the Mount: The Beatitudes" (video), ChurchofJesusChrist.org.

MATTHEW 5:13

"Ye are the salt of the earth."

Salt has long been used to preserve, flavor, and purify. Salt also had religious meaning for the Israelites. It was associated with the ancient practice of animal sacrifice under the law of Moses (see Leviticus 2:13; Numbers 18:19). When salt loses its savor, it becomes ineffective, or "good for nothing" (Matthew 5:13). This happens when it is mixed with or contaminated by other elements.

Keep this in mind as you ponder Matthew 5:13. How will you keep your savor as a disciple of Jesus Christ? How will you fulfill your preserving and purifying work as the salt of the earth?

See also Doctrine and Covenants 103:9–10.

"Ye are the salt of the earth" (Matthew 5:13).

MATTHEW 5:17–48; LUKE 6:27–35

The law of Christ supersedes the law of Moses.

The disciples may have been surprised to hear Jesus say that their righteousness needed to exceed that of the scribes and Pharisees (see Matthew 5:20), who prided themselves on how well they kept the law of Moses.

As you read Matthew 5:21–48 and Luke 6:27–35, consider marking both the behaviors required in the law of Moses ("Ye have heard that . . .") and what Jesus taught to elevate these behaviors. Why do you think the Savior's way is a higher law?

For example, what did Jesus teach in Matthew 5:27–28 about our responsibility over our thoughts? How can you gain more control over the thoughts and feelings that come into your mind and heart? (see Doctrine and Covenants 121:45).

See also "Sermon on the Mount: The Higher Law" (video), ChurchofJesusChrist.org.

MATTHEW 5:48

Does Heavenly Father really expect me to be perfect?

President Russell M. Nelson taught:

"The term *perfect* was translated from the Greek *teleios*, which means 'complete.' . . . The infinitive form of the verb is *teleiono*, which means 'to reach a distant end, to be fully developed, to consummate, or to finish.' Please note that the word does not imply 'freedom from error'; it implies 'achieving a distant objective.' . . .

". . . The Lord taught, 'Ye are not able to abide the presence of God now . . . ; wherefore, continue in patience until ye are perfected' [Doctrine and Covenants 67:13].

"We need not be dismayed if our earnest efforts toward perfection now seem so arduous and endless. Perfection is pending. It can come in full only after the Resurrection and only through the Lord. It awaits all who love him and keep his commandments" ("Perfection Pending," *Ensign*, Nov. 1995, 86, 88).

See also 2 Peter 1:3–11; Moroni 10:32–33; Doctrine and Covenants 76:69; Jeffrey R. Holland, "Be Ye Therefore Perfect—Eventually," *Ensign* or *Liahona*, Nov. 2017, 40–42.

 ## Ideas for Family Scripture Study and Home Evening

Matthew 5:1–9. Which principles taught in Matthew 5:1–9 could help your home be a happier place? You might choose one or two that seem especially important to your family. For example, what teachings do we find that can help us be peacemakers? (see Matthew 5:21–25, 38–44). What goals can we set? How will we follow up?

Matthew 5:13. Eat together some food seasoned with salt and the same food without salt. What difference do we notice? What does it mean to be "the salt of the earth"? How can we do this?

Matthew 5:14–16. To help your family understand what it means to be "the light of the world," you could explore some of the sources of light in your home, your neighborhood, and the world. It might be helpful to show what happens when you hide a light. What did Jesus mean when He said, "Ye are the light of the world"? (Matthew 5:14). Who has been like a light for our family? How can we be a light to others? (see 3 Nephi 18:16, 24–25).

Matthew 5:43–45. As your family reads the Savior's words in these verses, you might talk about who, specifically, you feel you could love, bless, and pray for. How can we increase our love for them?

For more ideas for teaching children, see this week's outline in *Come, Follow Me—For Primary*.

Suggested song: "Shine On," *Children's Songbook*, 144.

Improving Our Teaching

Be observant. "As you pay attention to what is happening in your [children's] lives, you will find excellent teaching opportunities. . . . Comments that [they] make or questions they ask can also lead to teaching moments" (*Teaching in the Savior's Way*, 16).

"Ye are the light of the world" (Matthew 5:14).

Jesus Teaching the People by the Seashore, by James Tissot

Matthew 6–7

"HE TAUGHT THEM AS ONE HAVING AUTHORITY"

When we read the scriptures with a question in mind and with a sincere desire to understand what Heavenly Father wants us to know, we invite the Holy Ghost to inspire us. As you read Matthew 6–7, pay attention to these impressions.

RECORD YOUR IMPRESSIONS

The Sermon on the Mount is one of the best-known discourses in Christianity. The Savior taught with rich images, such as a city set on a hill, lilies of the field, and wolves disguised as sheep. But the Sermon on the Mount is far more than a beautiful speech. The power of the Savior's teachings to His disciples can change our lives, especially when we live by them. Then His words become more than words; they become a sure foundation for life that, like the wise man's house, can withstand the world's winds and floods (see Matthew 7:24–25).

 Ideas for Personal Scripture Study

MATTHEW 6–7

Living the Savior's teachings can help me become like Him.

The Sermon on the Mount contains many gospel principles. As you study these chapters, ask the Lord what He wants you to learn.

One principle you might find is the need to prioritize the things of God over the things of the world. Which of the Savior's teachings in Matthew 6–7 help you focus on heavenly things? What other thoughts or impressions do you have? What are you inspired to do? Consider recording your impressions. For example:

Matthew 6:1–4	I want to care more about what God thinks of me than what others think.

Another principle in Matthew 6–7 is prayer. Take a moment to evaluate your prayers. How do you feel you are doing in your efforts to draw closer to God through prayer? What teachings in Matthew 6–7 inspire you to improve how you pray? Record the impressions you receive. For example:

Matthew 6:9	When I pray, I want to treat Heavenly Father's name with reverence.
Matthew 6:10	When I pray, I can express my desire that the Lord's will be done.

You might consider reading the Sermon on the Mount again, looking for other recurring principles or messages that are especially applicable to you. Record what you find in a study journal, along with your thoughts and impressions.

What does it mean to use "vain repetitions" in prayer?

People often understand "vain repetitions" to mean repeating the same words over and over again. However, the word *vain* can describe something that has no value. Using "vain repetitions" in prayer can mean praying without sincere, heartfelt feeling (see Alma 31:12–23).

We can draw closer to God through prayer.

I can judge righteously.

In Matthew 7:1, the Savior may seem to be saying we should never judge, but in other scriptures (including other verses in this chapter), He gives us instructions about how to judge. If that seems puzzling, the Joseph Smith Translation of this verse might help: "Judge not *unrighteously*, that ye be not judged; *but judge righteous judgment*" (in Matthew 7:1, footnote *a*). What do you find in Matthew 7:1–5, along with the rest of the chapter, that helps you know how to "judge righteous judgment"?

See also Gospel Topics, "Judging Others," topics.ChurchofJesusChrist.org; Lynn G. Robbins, "The Righteous Judge," *Ensign* or *Liahona*, Nov. 2016, 96–98.

I come to know Jesus Christ by doing His will.

The phrase "I never knew you" in Matthew 7:23 was changed in the Joseph Smith Translation to "Ye never knew me" (Matthew 7:23, footnote *a*). How does this change help you better understand what the Lord taught in verses 21–22 about doing His will? How well do you feel you know the Lord? What can you do to know Him better?

See also David A. Bednar, "If Ye Had Known Me," *Ensign* or *Liahona*, Nov. 2016, 102–5.

Obeying the Savior's teachings creates a firm foundation for my life.

Living the gospel doesn't remove adversity from our lives. Both houses in the Savior's parable in Matthew 7:24–27 experienced the same storm. But one of the houses was able to withstand it. How has living the Savior's teachings created a solid foundation for you? What do you feel inspired to do to continue building your "house upon a rock"? (see verse 24).

See also Helaman 5:12.

 Ideas for Family Scripture Study and Home Evening

Matthew 6–7. One way to learn from Matthew 6–7 as a family is to watch the videos "Sermon on the Mount: The Lord's Prayer" and "Sermon on the Mount: Treasures in Heaven" (ChurchofJesusChrist.org). Family members could follow along in their scriptures and pause the videos whenever they hear something they want to discuss. This activity could span several days, if needed.

Matthew 6:5–13. What can we learn about prayer from the way the Savior prayed? How can we use His prayer as a model to improve our personal and family prayers? (See also Luke 11:1–13.) If you have younger children, you might practice praying together.

Matthew 6:33. What does it mean to "seek . . . first the kingdom of God"? How are we doing this individually and as a family?

Matthew 7:1–5. To visualize the teachings in these verses, your family could find a mote (a tiny wood fragment) and a beam (a large piece of wood). What does comparing the two teach us about judging others? If you'd like to explore this topic further, you could use some of the resources in "Judging Others" (Gospel Topics, topics.ChurchofJesusChrist.org).

Matthew 7:24–27. To help your family better understand the Savior's parable of the wise man and the foolish man, you could let them pour water on sand and then on a rock. How can we build our spiritual foundations on a rock?

For more ideas for teaching children, see this week's outline in *Come, Follow Me—For Primary*.

Suggested song: "The Wise Man and the Foolish Man," *Children's Songbook*, 281.

Improving Personal Study

Share insights. Discussing principles you learn from your personal study is not only a good way to teach others; it also helps strengthen your own understanding. Try sharing a principle you learned this week with a family member or in your Church classes.

Have Prayed for Thee, by Del Parson

Matthew 8; Mark 2–4; Luke 7

"THY FAITH HATH SAVED THEE"

Be careful not to rush your study of the scriptures. Take time for prayerful pondering, even if it means you don't have time to read every verse. These moments of pondering often lead to personal revelation.

RECORD YOUR IMPRESSIONS

One of the clearest messages in the New Testament is that Jesus Christ is a healer. Accounts of the Savior healing the sick and afflicted are many—from a woman with a fever to a widow's son who had died. Why the emphasis on physical healing? What messages might there be for us in these miracles? Certainly one obvious message is that Jesus Christ is the Son of God, with power over all things, including our physical pains and imperfections. But another meaning is found in His words to the skeptical scribes: "That ye may know that the Son of man hath power on earth to forgive sins" (Mark 2:10). So when you read about a blind person or a leper being healed, you might think of the healing—both spiritual and physical—that you can receive from the Savior and hear Him say to you, "Thy faith hath saved thee" (Luke 7:50).

 Ideas for Personal Scripture Study

MATTHEW 8; MARK 2–3; LUKE 7

The Savior can heal infirmities and sicknesses.

These few chapters record many instances of miraculous healings performed by the Savior. As you study these healings, look for possible messages for you. You might ask yourself: What does the account teach about faith in Jesus Christ? What does the account teach about the

Savior? What does God want me to learn from this miracle? Here are some examples, but there are many more:

- A leper (Matthew 8:1–4)

- A centurion's servant (Matthew 8:5–13; Luke 7:1–10)

- Peter's mother-in-law (Matthew 8:14–15)

- A man sick with palsy (Mark 2:1–12)

- A man with a withered hand (Mark 3:1–5)

- The son of the widow of Nain (Luke 7:11–16)

See also David A. Bednar, "Accepting the Lord's Will and Timing," *Ensign*, Aug. 2016, 29–35, or *Liahona*, Aug. 2016, 17–23; Neil L. Andersen, "Wounded," *Ensign* or *Liahona*, Nov. 2018, 83–86.

MARK 2:15–17; LUKE 7:36–50

Jesus Christ came not to condemn sinners but to heal them.

As you read in these verses about Jesus's interactions with scribes and Pharisees, you might consider whether you see yourself in these accounts. For example, are your thoughts and actions ever like those of Simon the Pharisee? How would you describe the difference between the way Jesus saw sinners and the way Pharisees like Simon saw them? Consider how those who are weighed down by sin might feel when they are with the Savior. How do they feel when they are with you?

You might also ponder how you are like the woman described in Luke 7:36–50. When have you experienced the tenderness and mercy that the Savior showed her? What do you learn from her example of faith, love, and humility?

See also John 3:17; Luke 9:51–56; Dieter F. Uchtdorf, "The Gift of Grace," *Ensign* or *Liahona*, May 2015, 107–10.

MATTHEW 8:18–22; MARK 3:31–35

Being a disciple of Jesus Christ means that I put Him first in my life.

In these verses, Jesus taught that being His disciples requires us to put Him first in our lives, even if that sometimes means we must sacrifice other things that we value. As you study these passages, ponder your own discipleship. Why must disciples be willing to put the Savior first? What might you need to give up in order to put Jesus first? (See also Luke 9:57–62.)

MATTHEW 8:23–27; MARK 4:35–41

Jesus Christ has power to bring peace in the midst of life's storms.

Have you ever felt the way Jesus's disciples did in the storm at sea—watching the waves of water fill the boat and questioning, "Master, carest thou not that we perish?"

In Mark 4:35–41, you will find four questions. List each one, and ponder what it teaches you about facing life's challenges with faith in Jesus Christ. How does the Savior bring peace to the storms of your life?

See also Lisa L. Harkness, "Peace, Be Still," *Ensign* or *Liahona*, Nov. 2020, 80–82.

From Fear to Faith, by Howard Lyon

Ideas for Family Scripture Study and Home Evening

Matthew 8; Mark 2–4; Luke 7. Consider creating a list of the miracles described in these chapters. Try finding or drawing pictures of some of them (see the *Gospel Art Book* or ChurchofJesusChrist .org). Each family member could use pictures to tell about one of the miracles and share what they learn from it. You might share some examples of miracles you have seen or read about in our day.

See also the videos "Widow of Nain" and "Calming the Tempest" (ChurchofJesusChrist.org).

Matthew 8:5–13; Luke 7:1–10. What was it about the centurion's faith that impressed Jesus? How can we show similar faith in Jesus Christ?

Mark 2:1–12. "Chapter 23: The Man Who Could Not Walk" (in *New Testament Stories*, 57–58, or the corresponding video on ChurchofJesusChrist.org) could help your family discuss Mark 2:1–12. (See also the video "Jesus Forgives Sins and Heals a Man Stricken with Palsy" on ChurchofJesusChrist.org.) How can we be like the friends of the man who could not walk? Who has been that kind of friend to us?

Mark 4:35–41. Could this account help family members when they feel afraid? Perhaps they could read verse 39 and share experiences when the Savior helped them feel peace.

Children might enjoy pretending they are in a boat in a stormy sea while someone reads Mark 4:35–38. Then, when someone reads verse 39, they could pretend to be in a boat in a calm sea. You could also sing together a song about finding peace in the Savior, such as "Master, the Tempest Is Raging" (*Hymns*, no. 105). What phrases in the song teach us about the peace Jesus offers?

For more ideas for teaching children, see this week's outline in *Come, Follow Me—For Primary*.

Suggested hymn: "Master, the Tempest Is Raging," *Hymns*, no. 105.

Improving Our Teaching

Be available and accessible. Some of the best teaching moments start as questions or concerns in the hearts of family members. Let family members know through your words and actions that you are eager to hear them. (See *Teaching in the Savior's Way*, 16.)

Christ and the Palsied Man, by J. Kirk Richards

Matthew 9–10; Mark 5; Luke 9

"THESE TWELVE JESUS SENT FORTH"

The study ideas in this outline are meant to help you find personal meaning in the scriptures. They should not, however, replace personal revelation you might receive about what passages to study or how to study them.

RECORD YOUR IMPRESSIONS

Word of Jesus's healing miracles was spreading quickly. Multitudes followed Him, hoping for relief from their sicknesses. But when the Savior looked upon the multitudes, He saw more than their physical ailments. Filled with compassion, He saw "sheep having no shepherd" (Matthew 9:36). "The harvest truly is plenteous," He observed, "but the labourers are few" (Matthew 9:37). So He called twelve Apostles, "gave them power," and sent them to teach and minister "to the lost sheep of the house of Israel" (Matthew 10:1, 6). Today the need for more laborers to serve Heavenly Father's children is just as great. There are still twelve Apostles, but there are more disciples of Jesus Christ than ever before—people who can declare to all the world, "The kingdom of heaven is at hand" (Matthew 10:7).

Ideas for Personal Scripture Study

MATTHEW 9:18–26; MARK 5:22–43

"Be not afraid, only believe."

When Jairus first asked Jesus to heal his daughter, who was "at the point of death," Jairus spoke urgently but hopefully: "Come and lay thy hands on her, . . . and she shall live" (Mark 5:23). But as they went, a messenger told Jairus that it was too late: "Thy daughter is dead: why troublest thou the Master any further?" (verse 35). Likewise, it might have seemed too late for the woman described in Mark 5:25–34, who had suffered with an ailment for 12 years.

As you read these accounts, you might think of things that need healing in your life or your family—including things that might seem "at the point of death" or too late for healing. What impresses you about the expressions of faith in these accounts? Note also what Jesus says to the woman and to Jairus. What do you feel He is saying to you?

See also Luke 8:41–56; Russell M. Nelson, "Drawing the Power of Jesus Christ into Our Lives," *Ensign* or *Liahona*, May 2017, 39–42; *Teachings of Presidents of the Church: Gordon B. Hinckley* (2016), 333–42.

Trust in the Lord, by Liz Lemon Swindle

MATTHEW 10; LUKE 9:1–6

The Lord gives His servants power to do His work.

The instructions Jesus gave in Matthew 10 to His Apostles can apply to us as well, because we all have a part in the Lord's work. What power did Christ give His Apostles to help them fulfill their mission? How can you access His power in the work you have been called to do? (see 2 Corinthians 6:1–10; Doctrine and Covenants 121:34–46).

As you read the commission Christ gave to His Apostles, you might receive impressions about the work the Lord wants you to do. A chart like the following could help you organize your thoughts:

Matthew 10	Impressions I receive
The Savior gave His disciples power.	God will give me the power I need to do my work.

See also Mark 6:7–13; Articles of Faith 1:6; Bible Dictionary, "Apostle"; "Jesus Calls Twelve Apostles to Preach and Bless Others" (video), ChurchofJesusChrist.org.

MATTHEW 10:17–20

When I am in the Lord's service, He will inspire me with what to say.

The Lord foresaw that His disciples would be persecuted and questioned about their faith—something similar to what disciples today may experience. But He promised the disciples that they would know by the Spirit what to say. Have you had experiences when this divine promise was fulfilled in your life, perhaps when you bore your testimony, gave a blessing, or had a conversation with someone? Consider sharing your experiences with a loved one or recording them in a journal. What do you feel inspired to do so that you can have such experiences more often?

See also Luke 12:11–12; Doctrine and Covenants 84:85.

MATTHEW 10:34–39

What did Jesus mean by "I came not to send peace, but a sword"?

Elder D. Todd Christofferson taught: "I'm confident that a number of you have been rejected and ostracized by father and mother, brothers and sisters as you accepted the gospel of Jesus Christ and entered into His covenant. In one way or another, your superior love of Christ has required the sacrifice of relationships that were dear to you, and you have shed many tears. Yet with your own love undiminished, you hold steady under this cross, showing yourself unashamed of the Son of God" ("Finding Your Life," *Ensign*, Mar. 2016, 28).

This willingness to lose cherished relationships in order to follow the Savior comes with a promise that "he that loseth his life for my sake shall find it" (Matthew 10:39).

Ideas for Family Scripture Study and Home Evening

Mark 5:22–43. As your family reads this story together, you might pause to ask family members how they might feel if they were Jairus, the woman, or other people in the story. You could also show pictures of the story, such as those in this outline. How do these pictures depict the faith of the people in the stories? (See also the videos "Jesus Raises the Daughter of Jairus" and "Jesus Heals a Woman of Faith" on ChurchofJesusChrist.org.) You might also consider some challenges your family faces. How can we apply His words, "Be not afraid, only believe"? (Mark 5:36).

Matthew 10:39; Luke 9:23–26. What might it mean to "lose" our life and to "find" it? (Matthew 10:39). Perhaps family members could share experiences that illustrate Jesus's teachings in these verses.

Matthew 10:40. How are you and your family doing at receiving and following the counsel of modern-day Apostles? How is our obedience to their counsel bringing us closer to Jesus Christ?

Luke 9:61–62. What does it mean to look back after putting our hand to the plow? Why would this attitude make us not fit for the kingdom of God?

For more ideas for teaching children, see this week's outline in *Come, Follow Me—For Primary.*

Suggested hymn: "When Faith Endures," *Hymns,* no. 128.

Improving Personal Study

Listen to the Spirit. As you study, pay attention to your thoughts and feelings (see Doctrine and Covenants 8:2–3), even if they seem unrelated to what you are reading. Those impressions may be the very things God wants you to know and do.

Talitha Cumi, by Eva Koleva Timothy

Matthew 11–12; Luke 11

"I WILL GIVE YOU REST"

President Dallin H. Oaks taught: "The scriptures, which are the revelations of the past, cannot be understood without openness to the revelations of the present. . . . A study of the scriptures enables men and women to receive revelations" ("Scripture Reading and Revelation," *Ensign*, Jan. 1995, 7).

RECORD YOUR IMPRESSIONS

In many ways, the Pharisees and scribes had made worshipping Jehovah burdensome. They often emphasized strict rules over eternal truths. Rules about the Sabbath day, which was meant to be a day of rest, were themselves a heavy burden.

And then, Jehovah Himself came among His people. He taught them that the true purpose of religion is not to create burdens but to relieve them. He taught that God gives us commandments, including the one to honor the Sabbath, not to oppress us but to bless us. Yes, the way to God is strait and narrow, but the Lord came to announce that we need not walk it alone. "Come unto me," He pleaded. His invitation, to all who feel "heavy laden" for any reason, is to stand beside Him, to bind ourselves to Him, and to let Him share our burdens. His promise is "Ye shall find rest unto your souls." Compared to the alternatives—trying to carry on alone or relying on mortal solutions—His "yoke is easy, and [His] burden is light" (Matthew 11:28–30).

Ideas for Personal Scripture Study

Jesus Christ will give me rest as I rely on Him.

We all carry burdens—some resulting from our own sins and mistakes, some caused by the choices of others, and some that are nobody's fault but are simply part of life on earth. Regardless of the reasons for our struggles, Jesus pleads with us to come unto Him so He can help us bear our burdens and find relief (see also Mosiah 24). Elder David A. Bednar taught, "Making and keeping sacred covenants yokes us to and with the Lord Jesus Christ" ("Bear Up Their Burdens with Ease," *Ensign* or *Liahona*, May 2014, 88). With this in mind, ponder questions like the following to better understand the Savior's words in these verses: How do my covenants yoke me to and with the Savior? What do I need to do to come unto Christ? In what sense is the Savior's yoke easy and His burden light?

What other questions come to your mind as you read? Record them, and search for answers this week in the scriptures and the words of the prophets. You may find answers to some of your questions in Elder David A. Bednar's message referenced above.

See also John A. McCune, "Come unto Christ—Living as Latter-day Saints," *Ensign* or *Liahona*, May 2020, 36–38; Lawrence E. Corbridge, "The Way," *Ensign* or *Liahona*, Nov. 2008, 34–36.

The Disciples Eat Wheat on the Sabbath, by James Tissot

MATTHEW 12:1–13

"Do well on the sabbath days."

The teachings of the Pharisees differed from the Savior's in many ways, but especially in how to honor the Sabbath day. As you read Matthew 12:1–13, you might consider how well your attitudes and actions regarding the Sabbath align with the Savior's teachings. To do this, you could ponder statements like these:

- "I will have mercy, and not sacrifice" (verse 7; see Hosea 6:6).

- "The Son of man is Lord even of the sabbath day" (verse 8).

- "It is lawful to do well on the sabbath days" (verse 12).

How might these teachings influence the way you approach the Sabbath?

See also Mark 2:23–3:5; Gospel Topics, "Sabbath Day," topics.ChurchofJesusChrist.org.

My words and actions reflect what is in my heart.

One of the Savior's main criticisms of the Pharisees was that they tried to appear righteous but their intentions were not pure. As you study the Savior's warnings to the Pharisees in Matthew 12:34–37 and Luke 11:33–44, ponder the connection between our hearts and our actions. What does the phrase "good treasure of the heart" mean to you? (Matthew 12:35). How do our words justify or condemn us? (see Matthew 12:37). What might it mean for your eye to be "single"? (Luke 11:34). Ponder how you can become "full of light" (Luke 11:36) through the Savior's power.

See also Alma 12:12–14; Doctrine and Covenants 88:67–68.

 ## Ideas for Family Scripture Study and Home Evening

Matthew 11:28–30. You can help your family visualize the Savior's teachings in these verses by having them take turns trying to pull something heavy, first by themselves and then with help. What are some of the burdens we carry? What does it mean to take Christ's yoke upon ourselves? The picture at the end of this outline could help you explain what a yoke is.

Matthew 12:10–13. As you read about Jesus healing a man on the Sabbath, your family could talk about how we are "restored whole" by the Savior. How can the Sabbath be a day of healing for us?

Inspired by the Savior's example in these verses, your family could make a list of ways you can "do well on the sabbath" (verse 12). Be sure to include opportunities to serve others. It could be helpful to keep your list and refer to it on future Sundays.

Luke 11:33–36. Ponder how you might teach your family what it means to be "full of light" (verses 34, 36). Would an object lesson help? You could also discuss ways to bring the Savior's light into our lives, our home, and the world. For ideas, see the video "The Light That Shineth in Darkness," ChurchofJesusChrist.org.

Luke 11:37–44. Perhaps your family could discuss these verses while washing dishes together. You could talk about why it would be a bad idea to wash only the outsides of things like bowls and cups. You could then relate this to the need to be righteous not just in our outward deeds but also in our inward thoughts and feelings.

For more ideas for teaching children, see this week's outline in *Come, Follow Me—For Primary*.

Suggested hymn: "How Gentle God's Commands," *Hymns*, no. 125.

Improving Personal Study

Be consistent. You may have days when studying the scriptures seems more difficult or less impactful than you hoped. Don't give up. Elder David A. Bednar taught, "Our consistency in doing seemingly small things can lead to significant spiritual results" ("More Diligent and Concerned at Home," *Ensign* or *Liahona*, Nov. 2009, 20).

"Take my yoke upon you, and learn of me; for I am meek and lowly in heart: and ye shall find rest unto your souls" (Matthew 11:29).
Photograph © iStockphoto.com/wbritten

Matthew 13; Luke 8; 13

"WHO HATH EARS TO HEAR, LET HIM HEAR"

As you read Matthew 13 and Luke 8; 13, think about how you will prepare yourself to "hear" and appreciate the Savior's teachings in these parables. What will you do to apply these teachings in your life?

RECORD YOUR IMPRESSIONS

Some of the Savior's most memorable teachings were in the form of simple stories called parables. These were more than just interesting anecdotes about ordinary objects or events. They contained profound truths about the kingdom of God for those who were spiritually prepared. One of the first parables recorded in the New Testament—the parable of the sower (see Matthew 13:3–23)—invites us to examine our readiness to receive God's word. "For whosoever receiveth," Jesus declared, "to him shall be given, and he shall have more abundance" (Joseph Smith Translation, Matthew 13:10 [in Matthew 13:12, footnote *a*]). So as we prepare to study the Savior's parables—or any of His teachings—a good place to start is to examine our hearts and determine whether we are giving the word of God "good ground" (Matthew 13:8) in which to grow, blossom, flourish, and produce fruit that will bless us and our families in abundance.

 Ideas for Personal Scripture Study

MATTHEW 13:3–23; LUKE 8:4–15; 13:6–9

My heart must be prepared to receive the word of God.

Why is it that sometimes our hearts are receptive to truth, while at other times we're tempted to resist it? Reading the parable of the sower can provide a good opportunity to think about how well you receive truth from the Lord. It might be helpful to match verses 3–8 of Matthew 13 with the interpretations provided in verses 18–23. What can you do to cultivate "good ground" in yourself? What might be some "thorns" that keep you from truly hearing and following God's word? How can you overcome these "thorns"?

Your study of this parable could also influence how you read the parable in Luke 13:6–9. What is the "fruit" that the Lord seeks from us? How do we nourish our ground so we will "bear fruit"?

See also Mosiah 2:9; Alma 12:10–11; 32:28–43; Dallin H. Oaks, "The Parable of the Sower," *Ensign* or *Liahona*, May 2015, 32–35.

MATTHEW 13:24–35, 44–52; LUKE 13:18–21

Jesus's parables help me understand the growth and destiny of His Church.

The Prophet Joseph Smith taught that the parables in Matthew 13 describe the growth and destiny of the Church in the latter days. You might review the Prophet's words in *Teachings of Presidents of the Church: Joseph Smith* (2007), 293–303, as you consider what the following parables teach you about the Lord's Church:

- The wheat and the tares (13:24–30, 36–43)

- The mustard seed (13:31–32)

- The leaven (13:33)

- The hidden treasure and the pearl of great price (13:44–46)

- The net (13:47–50)

- The householder (13:52)

After pondering these parables, what do you feel inspired to do to participate more fully in the work of Christ's latter-day Church?

See also Guide to the Scriptures, "Kingdom of God or Kingdom of Heaven," "Parable," scriptures.ChurchofJesusChrist.org.

The gospel of Jesus Christ is a "pearl of great price" (Matthew 13:46).

MATTHEW 13:24–30, 36–43

The righteous must grow among the wicked until the end of the world.

One way to analyze this parable is to draw a picture of it and label it with the interpretations in Matthew 13:36–43 and Doctrine and Covenants 86:1–7. A tare is a "poisonous weed, which, until it comes into ear, is similar in appearance to wheat" (Bible Dictionary, "Tares"). What truths in this parable inspire you to remain faithful in spite of the wickedness in the world?

In what ways did "certain women" minister to the Savior?

"Female disciples traveled with Jesus and the Twelve, learning from [Jesus] spiritually and serving Him temporally. . . . In addition to receiving Jesus's ministering—the glad tidings of His gospel and the blessings of His healing power—these women ministered to Him, imparting their substance and devotion" (*Daughters in My Kingdom* [2017], 4). Women who followed the Savior also bore powerful testimony of Him (see Linda K. Burton, "Certain Women," *Ensign* or *Liahona*, May 2017, 12–15).

 Ideas for Family Scripture Study and Home Evening

Matthew 13. As your family members read the Savior's parables, they might enjoy thinking of their own parables that teach the same truths about the kingdom of heaven (the Church), using objects or situations that are familiar to them.

Matthew 13:3–23; Luke 8:4–15. After reading the parable of the sower together, your family might discuss questions like these: What can make our "ground" (our hearts) "stony" or "choke" the word? How can we make sure our ground is good and fruitful?

If you have younger children in your family, it could be fun to invite family members to act out different ways to prepare our hearts to hear the word of God while other family members guess what they are doing.

Matthew 13:13–16. How can you help your family members understand the importance of willingly receiving Christ's word? To demonstrate "ears [that] are dull of hearing," you might cover a family member's ears while you quietly read Matthew 13:13–16. How much did that family member understand from the verses? What are ways that we can open our eyes, ears, and hearts to the word of God?

Matthew 13:44–46. What do the two men in these parables have in common? Are there additional things we should be doing as individuals and as a family to put the kingdom of God first in our lives?

Luke 13:11–17. Have family members had experiences that caused them to feel that they could not "lift [themselves] up"? Do we know someone else who feels this way? How can we help? How does the Savior "loose" us from our infirmities?

For more ideas for teaching children, see this week's outline in *Come, Follow Me—For Primary*.

Suggested hymn: "We Are Sowing," *Hymns*, no. 216.

Improving Our Teaching

Memorize a scripture. Select a scripture passage that is particularly meaningful to your family, and invite family members to memorize it. Elder Richard G. Scott taught, "A memorized scripture becomes an enduring friend that is not weakened with the passage of time" ("The Power of Scripture," *Ensign* or *Liahona*, Nov. 2011, 6).

Parable of the Sower, by George Soper

Matthew 14; Mark 6; John 5–6

"BE NOT AFRAID"

As you read Matthew 14; Mark 6; and John 5–6, look for truths that are meaningful to you. You might ask yourself questions such as "How do the accounts in these chapters relate to me?" "What messages do I find for my life?" or "What would I like to share with my family or with others?"

RECORD YOUR IMPRESSIONS

What could have inspired Peter to leave the safety of his boat in the middle of the Sea of Galilee during a boisterous storm? What led him to believe that if Jesus could walk on water, he could too? We can't know for certain, but perhaps Peter understood that the Son of God came not just to do wonderful things for the people but to empower people like Peter to do wonderful things too. Jesus's invitation, after all, was "Come, follow me" (Luke 18:22). Peter had accepted this invitation once, and he was willing to accept it again, even if it meant facing his fears and doing something that seemed impossible. Perhaps the Lord will not ask us to step out of a boat in the middle of a storm or contribute our meager supply of bread when thousands need to eat, but He may ask us to accept directions even when we don't fully understand them. Whatever His invitations to us may be, they may sometimes seem surprising or even frightening. But miracles can happen if we, like Peter, will set aside our fears, our doubts, and our limited understanding and follow Him in faith.

Ideas for Personal Scripture Study

JOHN 5:16–47

Jesus Christ honors His Father.

The relationship between Heavenly Father and each of His children is meant to be a sacred one. In these verses, Jesus Christ gave us an inspiring model to follow in our relationship with Heavenly Father. Read John 5:16–47, and mark or note each instance of the word *Father*. How does the Son honor the Father, and how can you follow His example? What do you learn about how the Father feels about the Son? What are you inspired to do to strengthen your relationship with your Heavenly Father?

See also John 17; Jeffrey R. Holland, "The Grandeur of God," *Ensign* or *Liahona*, Nov. 2003, 70–73.

Jesus miraculously fed five thousand people with five loaves and two fishes.

MATTHEW 14:15–21; MARK 6:33–44; JOHN 6:5–14

The Savior can magnify my humble offerings to accomplish His purposes.

Have you ever felt inadequate to meet all the needs you see around you—in your home, in your relationships, or in society? Jesus's disciples must have felt inadequate when He asked them to feed over five thousand hungry people when there were only five loaves of bread and two fish available. As you read about the miracle that happened next, ponder how God might use your humble offerings of service to bless those around you. How has He magnified your efforts as you have served Him? Consider this statement from Sister Michelle D. Craig: "You and I can give what we have to Christ, and He will multiply our efforts. What you have to offer is more than enough—even with your human frailties and weaknesses—*if* you rely on the grace of God" ("Divine Discontent," *Ensign* or *Liahona*, Nov. 2018, 54).

MATTHEW 14:22–33; MARK 6:45–52; JOHN 6:15–21

Jesus Christ invites me to set aside my fears and doubts and exercise faith in Him.

Picture in your mind the details of the scene described in Matthew 14:22–33; Mark 6:45–52; and John 6:15–21. Imagine how Peter and the other disciples may have felt. What do you learn about discipleship from the Savior's words and actions in these verses? What do you learn from the words and actions of Peter? (See also 1 Nephi 3:7.) What is the Lord inviting you to do that might be like stepping out of the boat? What do you find in these verses that gives you courage to exercise your faith in Jesus Christ?

As a disciple of Jesus Christ, I must be willing to believe and accept the truth, even when it is hard to do.

When Jesus referred to Himself as the "bread of life" (John 6:48), many found this to be a "hard saying" (John 6:60). How can Peter's words in John 6:68–69 help you during times when the Savior's doctrine seems hard to accept or live by? What impresses you about Peter's testimony? What are some "words of eternal life" (John 6:68) that help you stay committed to following the Savior?

See also M. Russell Ballard, "To Whom Shall We Go?," *Ensign* or *Liahona*, Nov. 2016, 90–92.

 ## Ideas for Family Scripture Study and Home Evening

Matthew 14:15–21. Consider how you might help your family imagine how much bread and fish it would take to feed five thousand people. What does the miracle in Matthew 14:15–21 teach us about the Savior? Consider sharing an experience when you felt you didn't have enough to offer and the Savior multiplied your efforts.

Matthew 14:22–33. Your family might enjoy reenacting the story in these verses. Why would the disciples have been scared? Why was Peter able to overcome his fear and leave the boat? How did he show faith even when he began to sink? How are we sometimes like Peter?

John 5:1–16. Invite family members to note instances of the phrase "made whole" in these verses. In what ways can Jesus Christ make people whole? When and how has He made us whole?

John 6:28–58. Give each family member a piece of bread to eat, and discuss the benefits we receive from bread and other healthy foods. Then search these verses together, looking for why Jesus Christ called Himself the "bread of life" (John 6:35). What might it mean to "eat" the bread of life? (see D. Todd Christofferson, "The Living Bread Which Came Down from Heaven," *Ensign* or *Liahona*, Nov. 2017, 36–39).

For more ideas for teaching children, see this week's outline in *Come, Follow Me—For Primary*.

Suggested song: "How Great the Wisdom and the Love," *Hymns*, no. 195.

Improving Personal Study

Seek your own spiritual insights. In your personal and family study, do not limit yourself to the scripture passages addressed in these outlines. The Lord likely has messages for you in these chapters that are not covered here. Prayerfully seek them.

Against the Wind, by Liz Lemon Swindle

Easter

"O GRAVE, WHERE IS THY VICTORY?"

As you read the testimonies of the Savior's Resurrection in this outline, make note of the feelings and impressions that come to you from the Holy Ghost.

RECORD YOUR IMPRESSIONS

During the last week of the Savior's life, many Jews around Him were participating in the traditions of Passover. They prepared meals, sang songs, and gathered together to remember the deliverance of the house of Israel from slavery to the Egyptians. Families listened to the story of the destroying angel passing over the homes of their ancestors who had marked their doors with lamb's blood. Amid all these celebrations so rich with the symbolism of deliverance, relatively few were aware that Jesus Christ, the Lamb of God, was about to deliver them from the slavery of sin and death—through His suffering, His death, and His Resurrection. Even so, there were those who recognized Jesus as their promised Messiah, their eternal Deliverer. From that time onward, disciples of Jesus Christ have borne witness to all the world "that Christ died for our sins . . . ; and that he was buried, and that he rose again the third day" (1 Corinthians 15:3–4).

 Ideas for Personal Scripture Study

MATTHEW 21–28

Jesus Christ delivers me from sin and death, strengthens me in my weaknesses, and comforts me in my trials.

One way to focus on the blessings of the Savior's Atonement this week is to spend time each day reading about the last week of Jesus's life (a possible reading schedule follows). What do you find in these chapters that helps you feel the Savior's love? Ponder what these chapters teach you about how He can deliver you from sin, death, trials, and weaknesses. How are you exercising faith in His power of deliverance?

- Sunday: Triumphal entry into Jerusalem (Matthew 21:6–11)

- Monday: Cleansing the temple (Matthew 21:12–16)

- Tuesday: Teaching in Jerusalem (Matthew 21–23)

- Wednesday: Continued teaching (Matthew 24–25)

- Thursday: The Passover and Christ's suffering in the Garden of Gethsemane (Matthew 26)

- Friday: Trial, Crucifixion, and burial (Matthew 27:1–61)

- Saturday: Christ's body lies in the tomb (Matthew 27:62–66) while He ministers in the spirit world (Doctrine and Covenants 138)

- Sunday: Jesus Christ's Resurrection and appearance to His disciples (Matthew 28:1–10)

See also Easter.ComeuntoChrist.org.

Crucifixion, by Louise Parker

MATTHEW 28:1–10; LUKE 24:13–35; JOHN 20:19–29; 1 CORINTHIANS 15:1–8, 55

Many witnesses testify of the Resurrection of Jesus Christ.

Imagine what it would have been like for the disciples to watch Jesus being mocked, mistreated, and crucified. They had witnessed His power, felt the truth of His teachings, and had faith that He was the Son of God. Witnessing His death must have caused His disciples to feel grief and confusion. But soon they became witnesses of the great miracle of His Resurrection.

What can you learn from the accounts of those who witnessed the Resurrected Savior? Mark or note each person's experience in Matthew 28:1–10; Luke 24:13–35; John 20:19–29; and 1 Corinthians 15:1–8, 55. (Other witnesses of the resurrected Christ can be found in 3 Nephi 11; Mormon 1:15; Ether 12:38–39; Doctrine and Covenants 76:19–24; 110:1–10; and Joseph Smith— History 1:15–17.) What impresses you about the testimonies of these witnesses? After the Savior's Resurrection, others were resurrected and appeared to many (see Matthew 27:52–53; 3 Nephi 23:9). How does your faith in the Savior and the promise of resurrection influence the way you live?

See also "Jesus Is Resurrected," "The Risen Lord Appears to the Apostles," "Blessed Are They That Have Not Seen, and Yet Have Believed" (videos), ChurchofJesusChrist.org.

1 PETER 1:3–11

Jesus Christ gives me hope and joy.

What words or phrases in 1 Peter 1:3–11 give you hope because of Jesus Christ? When have you felt that hope?

Elder Gerrit W. Gong testified that the Resurrection "gives hope to those who have lost limbs; those who have lost ability to see, hear, or walk; or those thought lost to relentless disease, mental illness, or other diminished capacity. He finds us. He makes us whole. . . . [Also,] because 'God himself atoneth for the sins of the world' [Alma 42:15], . . . He can, with mercy, succor us according to our infirmities. . . . We repent and do all we can. He encircles us eternally 'in the arms of his love' [2 Nephi 1:15]" ("Hosanna and Hallelujah—The Living Jesus Christ: The Heart of Restoration and Easter," *Ensign* or *Liahona*, May 2020, 54).

See also Alma 27:28; 36:1–24; 3 Nephi 9:11–17; Moroni 7:40–41.

 Ideas for Family Scripture Study and Home Evening

ComeuntoChrist.org. Easter.ComeuntoChrist.org contains a timeline and description of what happened on each day of the last week of the Savior's life. Each day of the week, your family could review these descriptions to see what the Savior did that day, or you could read about His last week in the scriptures as a family (see a suggested list in "Ideas for Personal Scripture Study" above).

***Hymns* and *Children's Songbook*.** Consider singing songs together about the Savior's Atonement and Resurrection during this week, including some that are less familiar to you. (See the topics index of *Hymns* or *Children's Songbook*, under topics such as "Atonement," "Easter," or "Resurrection.") To help family members learn the songs, you could show pictures that go with the words.

"Jesus Christ" collection in Gospel Library. The Gospel Library collection titled "Jesus Christ" includes videos, artwork, and music that can help your family celebrate the Savior's Resurrection this Easter.

"The Living Christ: The Testimony of the Apostles." As a family, read "The Living Christ: The Testimony of the Apostles" (ChurchofJesusChrist.org). Invite each family member to pick an Easter message from this testimony to share with others. For example, you might create posters to display on social media, on your front door, or in your home.

For more ideas for teaching children, see this week's outline in *Come, Follow Me—For Primary*.

Suggested song: "Jesus Has Risen," *Children's Songbook*, 70.

Improving Personal Study

Set manageable goals. Spending even a few minutes a day studying the scriptures can bless your life. Commit to studying each day, find a way to remind yourself of your commitment, and do your best to follow through. If you forget, don't give up. Just start again.

Gethsemane, by Adam Abram

Matthew 15–17; Mark 7–9

"THOU ART THE CHRIST"

Reading the scriptures invites the Holy Ghost into your life. One of the Holy Ghost's important missions is to testify of Jesus Christ. As you read the scriptures this week, pay attention to spiritual feelings that strengthen your testimony of the Savior.

RECORD YOUR IMPRESSIONS

Isn't it strange that the Pharisees and Sadducees would demand that Jesus show them "a sign from heaven"? Weren't His many well-known miracles enough? What about His powerful teachings or the multiple ways He had fulfilled ancient prophecies? Their demand was prompted not by a lack of signs but by an unwillingness to "discern the signs" and accept them. (See Matthew 16:1–4.)

Peter, like the Pharisees and Sadducees, witnessed the Savior's miracles and heard His teachings. But Peter's definitive testimony, "Thou art the Christ, the Son of the living God," did not come through his physical senses—his "flesh and blood." His testimony was revealed to him by our "Father which is in heaven." *Revelation* is the rock upon which the Savior built His Church then and now—revelation from heaven to His servants. And this is the rock upon which we can build our discipleship—revelation that Jesus is the Christ and that His servants hold "the keys of the kingdom." When we are built upon this foundation, "the gates of hell shall not prevail against [us]" (Matthew 16:15–19).

Ideas for Personal Scripture Study

MATTHEW 16:13–17

A testimony of Jesus Christ comes by revelation.

If Jesus Christ asked people today, "Whom do men say that I the Son of Man am?" what might they say? How would you respond if Jesus asked you, "Whom say ye that I am?" (See Matthew 16:13–15.)

Ponder your testimony of the Savior and how you received it. What do you learn from Matthew 16:15–17 that could strengthen it? If you would like to learn more about testimony and personal revelation, explore these scriptures: John 15:26; 2 Nephi 31:17–18; Alma 5:45–48; and Doctrine and Covenants 8:2–3.

See also "President Nelson: Hear Him—Personal Revelation" (video), ChurchofJesusChrist.org.

MATTHEW 16:13–19; 17:1–9; MARK 9:2–9

"The keys of the kingdom of heaven" are on the earth today.

The "keys of the kingdom of heaven" that the Savior promised to give Peter are priesthood keys (Matthew 16:19). What are priesthood keys? Why do we need them? Ponder these questions as you read about the Savior's promise in Matthew 16:13–19 and its fulfillment in Matthew 17:1–9; Mark 9:2–9 (see also Joseph Smith Translation, Mark 9:3 [in Mark 9:4, footnote *a*]).

Other resources to help you learn about priesthood keys include Doctrine and Covenants 65:2; 107:18–20; 110:11–16; 128:9–11; "Keys of the Priesthood" in Guide to the Scriptures (scriptures.ChurchofJesusChrist.org); and Elder Gary E. Stevenson's message "Where Are the Keys and Authority of the Priesthood?," (*Ensign* or *Liahona*, May 2016, 29–32). While studying these resources, consider making a list of what you learn about priesthood keys and the blessings that come from them. Why do you think a key is a good symbol for the right to direct priesthood service?

See also Dallin H. Oaks, "The Melchizedek Priesthood and the Keys," *Ensign* or *Liahona*, May 2020, 69–72; Bible Dictionary, "Transfiguration, Mount of."

Priesthood keys are the authority to direct the use of the priesthood.

MATTHEW 17:14–21; MARK 9:14–29

When seeking greater faith, I can start with the faith I have.

The father mentioned in Matthew 17 and Mark 9 had reasons to feel uncertain that Jesus could heal his son. He had asked Jesus's disciples to heal his son, and they could not. But when he asked the Savior for a miracle, he chose to express faith. "Lord, I believe," he said. Then, in acknowledgment that his faith was not perfect, he added, "Help thou mine unbelief."

What does the Spirit teach you as you read about this miracle? How has Heavenly Father helped you increase your faith? What can you do to build upon the faith you already have? Perhaps you could compile a list of scriptures, conference messages, or experiences that have strengthened your faith.

See also Jeffrey R. Holland, "Lord, I Believe," *Ensign* or *Liahona*, May 2013, 93–95.

 ## Ideas for Family Scripture Study and Home Evening

Matthew 15:7–9; Mark 7:6–7. What is the difference between honoring God with our lips, or words, and honoring Him with our hearts?

Matthew 15:17–20; Mark 7:18–23. Why are we careful about what we put into our mouths? Based on what Jesus taught in these verses, why should we be even more careful about what comes out of our mouths—and out of our hearts? How can we keep our hearts pure?

Matthew 16:15–17. How does God reveal to us that Jesus is "the Christ, the Son of the living God"? (verse 16). How can we prepare ourselves to receive this revelation from Him?

Matthew 16:13–19; 17:1–9. To teach children about priesthood keys, you could tell Elder Gary E. Stevenson's story about getting locked out of his car (see the video "Where Are the Keys?" on ChurchofJesusChrist.org). You could let your children use keys to open the house, the car, or other locks. Consider showing a picture of the President of the Church and testifying that he holds all the priesthood keys, just as Peter did.

Matthew 17:20. Prophets with faith in Jesus Christ have moved literal mountains (see Jacob 4:6; Moses 7:13). But usually, that isn't the miracle we need. President M. Russell Ballard taught: "If we have faith as small as a mustard seed, the Lord can help us remove the mountains of discouragement and doubt in the tasks ahead of us as we serve with God's children, including family members, Church members, and those who are not yet members of the Church" ("Precious Gifts from God," *Ensign* or *Liahona*, May 2018, 10). What are some mountains in our lives that need to be moved? How can we show faith in God's power to help us remove these mountains?

For more ideas for teaching children, see this week's outline in *Come, Follow Me—For Primary*.

Suggested song: "I Believe in Christ," *Hymns*, no. 134.

Improving Our Teaching

Gather together often. President Henry B. Eyring taught: "Never miss a chance to gather children together to learn of the doctrine of Jesus Christ. Such moments are so rare in comparison with the efforts of the enemy" ("The Power of Teaching Doctrine," *Ensign*, May 1999, 74).

Master, I Have Brought unto Thee My Son, by Walter Rane

Matthew 18; Luke 10

"WHAT SHALL I DO TO INHERIT ETERNAL LIFE?"

As you prayerfully read and ponder Matthew 18 and Luke 10, pay attention to the quiet promptings of the Holy Ghost. He will tell you how these teachings and stories apply to you. Record the impressions you receive.

RECORD YOUR IMPRESSIONS

When you ask the Lord a question, you might receive an answer you did not expect. Who is my neighbor? Anyone who needs your help and love. Who is the greatest in the kingdom of heaven? A child. Is it enough to forgive an offender seven times? No, you should forgive seventy times seven. (See Luke 10:29–37; Matthew 18:4, 21–22.) Unexpected answers from the Lord can invite us to change the way we think, feel, and act. If you are seeking the Lord's will because you really want to learn from Him, the Lord will teach you how to live in a way that leads to eternal life with Him.

 Ideas for Personal Scripture Study

I must forgive others if I am to receive forgiveness from the Lord.

Peter's suggestion that he could forgive someone seven times might seem very generous, but Jesus taught a higher law. His response, "I say not unto thee, Until seven times: but, Until seventy times seven" (verse 22), was teaching not about numbers but rather about developing a Christlike attitude of forgiveness. As you read the parable of the unmerciful servant, ponder the times when you have felt God's mercy and compassion. Is there someone who needs to feel mercy and compassion from you?

Elder David E. Sorensen gave this important caution: "Although we must forgive a neighbor who injures us, we should still work constructively to prevent that injury from being repeated. . . . Forgiveness does not require us to accept or tolerate evil. . . . But as we fight against sin, we must not allow hatred or anger to control our thoughts or actions" ("Forgiveness Will Change Bitterness to Love," *Ensign* or *Liahona*, May 2003, 12).

LUKE 10:1–20

Who are the Seventy?

Following a pattern established in Old Testament times (see Exodus 24:1; Numbers 11:16), Jesus Christ "appointed other seventy," in addition to His Twelve Apostles, to witness of Him, preach His gospel, and assist Him in His work. This pattern continues in the restored Church. Seventies are called to assist the Twelve in their mission as special witnesses of Jesus Christ to all the world.

See also Doctrine and Covenants 107:25–26, 33–34, 97.

LUKE 10:25–37

To obtain eternal life, I must love God and love my neighbor as myself.

It is helpful to remember that the parable of the good Samaritan was Jesus's way of answering two questions: "What shall I do to inherit eternal life?" and "Who is my neighbour?" (Luke 10:25, 29). As you read this parable, keep these questions in mind. What answers do you find?

By Jesus's day, the animosity between the Jews and Samaritans had lasted for centuries. The Samaritans were descendants of Jews living in Samaria who had intermarried with Gentiles. The Jews felt that the Samaritans had become corrupted by their association with Gentiles and had apostatized. Jews would travel miles out of their way to avoid passing through Samaria. (See also Luke 9:52–54; 17:11–18; John 4:9; 8:48.)

Why do you think the Savior chose a Samaritan, someone who was hated by the Jews, as an example of compassion and loving one's neighbor? What does this parable inspire you to do?

See also Mosiah 2:17; "Parable of the Good Samaritan" and "A Good Samaritan" (videos), ChurchofJesusChrist.org.

LUKE 10:38–42

We choose "that good part" by making daily choices that lead to eternal life.

In Luke 10:38–42, Jesus gently invited Martha to think differently about the way she was spending her time. After quoting these verses, Sister Carol F. McConkie taught: "If we would be holy, we must learn to sit at the feet of the Holy One of Israel and give time to holiness. Do we set aside the phone, the never-ending to-do list, and the cares of worldliness? Prayer, study, and heeding the word of God invite His cleansing and healing love into our souls. Let us take time to be holy, that we may be filled with His sacred and sanctifying Spirit" ("The Beauty of Holiness," *Ensign* or *Liahona*, May 2017, 11). You may want to examine how you spend your time—even on good things. Is there something more "needful" (verse 42) that deserves more of your attention?

Ideas for Family Scripture Study and Home Evening

Matthew 18:1–11. Why would Jesus want us to become like a little child? What attributes do children have that we can develop to become more Christlike? (see Mosiah 3:19).

Jesus wants His disciples to become like little children.

Matthew 18:15. How can we apply the counsel in Matthew 18:15 to our family interactions? How would doing this bless our family?

Matthew 18:21–35. What does this parable teach us about Jesus Christ? What does it teach us about how to treat others?

Luke 10:25–37. Family members may enjoy wearing costumes and acting out this parable. How are we sometimes like the different people in the parable? How is the Savior like the good Samaritan? How can we be like the good Samaritan?

You might consider singing together a hymn or children's song that supports the truths in this parable. One example is "Lord, I Would Follow Thee" (*Hymns*, no. 220), but there are many others. Family members might enjoy finding a hymn or song and explaining how it relates to the parable.

Luke 10:38–42. Is it ever difficult to fit spiritual things into your family's schedule? The story of Mary and Martha could inspire a family council or home evening about how to do this better. As a family, you could make a list of ways to choose "that good part" (Luke 10:42).

For more ideas for teaching children, see this week's outline in *Come, Follow Me—For Primary*.

Suggested song: "Jesus Said Love Everyone," *Children's Songbook*, 61.

Improving Our Teaching

Nurture a loving atmosphere. The way family members feel about and treat each other can profoundly influence the spirit of your home. Help all family members do their part to establish a loving, respectful home so that everyone will feel safe sharing experiences, questions, and testimonies. (See *Teaching in the Savior's Way*, 15.)

Christ in the Home of Mary and Martha, by Walter Rane

John 7–10

"I AM THE GOOD SHEPHERD"

As you read John 7–10, you may receive impressions from the Holy Ghost about the doctrinal principles in these chapters. Recording your impressions can help you make a plan to act on them.

RECORD YOUR IMPRESSIONS

Although Jesus Christ came to bring "peace [and] good will toward men" (Luke 2:14), there was "a division among the people because of him" (John 7:43). People who witnessed the same events came to very different conclusions about who Jesus was. Some concluded, "He is a good man," while others said, "He deceiveth the people" (John 7:12). When He healed a blind man on the Sabbath, some insisted, "This man is not of God, because he keepeth not the sabbath day," while others asked, "How can a man that is a sinner do such miracles?" (John 9:16). Yet despite all the confusion, those who searched for truth recognized the power in His words, for "never man spake like this man" (John 7:46). When the Jews asked Jesus to "tell us plainly" whether he was the Christ, He revealed a principle that can help us distinguish truth from error: "My sheep hear my voice," He said, "and I know them, and they follow me" (John 10:24, 27).

 Ideas for Personal Scripture Study

JOHN 7:14–17

As I live the truths taught by Jesus Christ, I will come to know they are true.

The Jews marveled that Jesus knew so much, since He was not learned (see verse 15)—at least, not in ways they were familiar with. In Jesus's response, He taught a different way of knowing truth that is available to everyone, regardless of education or background. According to John 7:14–17, how can you come to know that the doctrine Jesus taught is true? How has this process helped you develop your testimony of the gospel?

JOHN 8:2–11

The Savior's mercy is available to all.

When speaking about the Savior's interaction with the woman taken in adultery, Elder Dale G. Renlund said: "Surely, the Savior did not condone adultery. But He also did not condemn the woman. He encouraged her to reform her life. She was motivated to change because of His compassion and mercy. The Joseph Smith Translation of the Bible attests to her resultant discipleship: 'And the woman glorified God from that hour, and believed on his name' [see John 8:11, footnote *c*]" ("Our Good Shepherd," *Ensign* or *Liahona*, May 2017, 30).

When have you felt like the woman, receiving mercy instead of condemnation from the Savior? When have you been like the scribes and Pharisees, accusing or judging others even when you are not without sin? (see John 8:7). What else can you learn from the way the Savior interacted with the scribes and Pharisees and the woman caught in adultery? What do you learn about the Savior's forgiveness as you read these verses?

See also "Go and Sin No More" (video), ChurchofJesusChrist.org.

JOHN 9

If we have faith, God can manifest Himself in our afflictions.

What does John 9:1–3 teach you about the challenges and afflictions of life? As you read John 9, ponder how the "works of God [were] made manifest" in the life of the man born blind. How have they been made manifest in your life—including in your afflictions?

JOHN 10:1–30

Jesus Christ is the Good Shepherd.

Even if you aren't familiar with sheep and shepherding, reading John 10, where the Savior says, "I am the good shepherd," can teach you important truths about Him. To find these truths, look for phrases that describe what a good shepherd is like and then consider how those phrases apply to the Savior. Below are some examples:

- Verse 3: "He calleth his own sheep by name, and leadeth them."

- Verse 11: He "giveth his life for the sheep."

- Verse 16: "There shall be one fold, and one shepherd."

Here are some additional questions to help you ponder this chapter: How is Jesus like a door? (see verses 7–9). How has He given you "life . . . more abundantly"? (verse 10). When have you felt that He knows you personally? (see verse 14). How do you recognize the Good Shepherd's voice? (see verse 27).

See also Psalm 23; Ezekiel 34; Alma 5:37–39; 3 Nephi 15:21–16:5; Gerrit W. Gong, "Good Shepherd, Lamb of God," *Ensign* or *Liahona*, May 2019, 97–101.

Ideas for Family Scripture Study and Home Evening

John 7:24. To help your family understand Jesus's teaching in John 7:24, you might show them something that looks one way on the outside but is different on the inside. Or family members could share experiences that taught them not to judge by outward appearances. You could also list qualities of each family member that aren't visible to the eye (see also 1 Samuel 16:7; Thomas S. Monson, "See Others as They May Become," *Ensign* or *Liahona*, Nov. 2012, 68–71).

John 8:31–36. What does it mean to be a "servant of sin"? (see also Moroni 7:11). What truths taught by Jesus can make us free?

Jesus Healing the Blind, by Carl Heinrich Bloch

John 9. How could you help your family visualize the account of Jesus healing the blind man in John 9? You could act out the story together or show the video "Jesus Heals a Man Born Blind" (ChurchofJesusChrist.org). Pause the story occasionally so that family members can read the corresponding verses from John 9. Invite them to note any lessons they learn from the account, such as what it means to become converted to the gospel of Jesus Christ.

John 10:1–18, 27–29. To involve family members in learning from the parable of the good shepherd, ask each of them to draw a picture of one of the following: a thief, a door, a shepherd, a hireling (a hired worker), a wolf, and a sheep. Invite them to read John 10:1–18, 27–29, and then discuss as a family what the Savior taught about the things they drew.

For more ideas for teaching children, see this week's outline in *Come, Follow Me—For Primary.*

Suggested hymn: "The Lord Is My Shepherd," *Hymns,* no. 108.

Improving Personal Study

Look for inspiring words and phrases. As you read, the Spirit may bring certain words or phrases to your attention that inspire and motivate you or seem to be written just for you. Consider making note of any words or phrases that inspire you in John 7–10.

Lost No More, by Greg K. Olsen

Luke 12–17; John 11

“REJOICE WITH ME; FOR I HAVE FOUND MY SHEEP WHICH WAS LOST”

As you read Luke 12–17 and John 11, prayerfully seek what Heavenly Father wants you to know and do. Your study of these chapters can open your heart to messages meant just for you.

RECORD YOUR IMPRESSIONS

In most situations, 99 out of 100 would be considered excellent—but not when such numbers stand for beloved children of God (see Doctrine and Covenants 18:10). In that case, even one soul merits a thorough, desperate search “until [we] find it” (Luke 15:4), as the Savior taught in the parable of the lost sheep. Then the rejoicing can begin, for “joy shall be in heaven over one sinner that repenteth, more than over ninety and nine just persons, which need no repentance” (Luke 15:7). If that seems unfair, it's helpful to remember that, in truth, there are none who “need no repentance.” We all need rescuing. And we all can participate in the rescue, rejoicing together over every soul who is saved (see Doctrine and Covenants 18:15–16).

 Ideas for Personal Scripture Study

LUKE 12; 14–16

I am blessed as I set my heart on eternal things.

Why would God say “Thou fool” to a hardworking, successful man who had built great barns and filled them with the fruits of his labors? (see Luke 12:16–21). In these chapters in Luke, the Savior teaches several parables that can help us lift our sights beyond the worldly to the eternal. Some of these parables are listed here. How would you summarize the message of each? What do you think the Lord is telling you?

- The foolish rich man (Luke 12:13–21)

- The great supper (Luke 14:12–24)

- The prodigal son (Luke 15:11–32)

- The unjust steward (Luke 16:1–12)

- The rich man and Lazarus (Luke 16:19–31)

See also Matthew 6:19–34; 2 Nephi 9:30; Doctrine and Covenants 25:10.

Heavenly Father rejoices when those who are lost are found.

As you read the parables Jesus taught in Luke 15, what do you learn about how Heavenly Father feels about those who have sinned or are otherwise "lost"? How should a spiritual leader—or any of us—feel toward them? Consider how the Pharisees and scribes would have answered these questions (see Luke 15:1–2). Jesus's response can be found in three parables in Luke 15. As you read, think about what Jesus was teaching the scribes and Pharisees with these parables.

You might also consider making a list of similarities and differences between the parables. For example, you could identify what was lost in each parable and why it was lost, how it was found, and how people reacted when it was found. What messages did Jesus have for those who are "lost"—including those who don't think they are lost? What messages did He have for people who seek those who are lost?

See also Doctrine and Covenants 18:10–16; Jeffrey R. Holland, "The Other Prodigal," *Ensign*, May 2002, 62–64.

The Lost Piece of Silver, by James Tissot

What was Christ teaching in the parable of the unjust steward?

Elder James E. Talmage explained one lesson we can learn from the parable: "Be diligent; for the day in which you can use your earthly riches will soon pass. Take a lesson from even the dishonest and the evil; if they are so prudent as to provide for the only future they think of, how much more should you, who believe in an eternal future, provide therefor! If you have not learned wisdom and prudence in the use of 'unrighteous mammon,' how can you be trusted with the more enduring riches?" (*Jesus the Christ* [1916], 464). What other lessons do you find in this parable?

Gratitude for my blessings will bring me closer to God.

If you had been one of the ten lepers, do you think you would have returned to thank the Savior? What additional blessings did the thankful leper receive because he gave thanks?

You might also ponder the Savior's words, "Thy faith hath made thee whole" (verse 19). In your opinion, how are gratitude and faith related? How do both help us become whole? The video "President Russell M. Nelson on the Healing Power of Gratitude" (ChurchofJesusChrist.org) can help you ponder these questions.

See also Dale G. Renlund, "Consider the Goodness and Greatness of God," *Ensign* or *Liahona*, May 2020, 41–44.

Jesus Christ is the Resurrection and the Life.

The miracle of raising Lazarus from the dead was a powerful and irrefutable testimony that Jesus was truly the Son of God and the promised Messiah. What words, phrases, or details in John 11:1–46 strengthen your faith that Jesus Christ is "the resurrection, and the life"? What does it mean to you that Jesus is "the resurrection, and the life"?

 Ideas for Family Scripture Study and Home Evening

Luke 15:1–10. Do your family members understand what it feels like to lose something—or to be lost? Talking about their experiences could start a discussion about the parables of the lost sheep and lost coin. Or you could play a game in which someone hides and other family members try to find him or her. How does this activity help us understand these parables?

Luke 15:11–32. How can we be like the father in this story when we have loved ones who are lost? What can we learn from the older son's experience that can help us be more Christlike? In what ways is the father in this parable like our Heavenly Father?

Luke 17:11–19. To help family members apply the account of the ten lepers, you could invite them to leave secret notes of gratitude for each other. You could also sing together "Count Your Blessings" (*Hymns*, no. 241) and count the blessings your family has received.

John 11:1–46. Family members could watch the video "Lazarus Is Raised from the Dead" (ChurchofJesusChrist.org) and share their testimonies of Jesus Christ.

For more ideas for teaching children, see this week's outline in *Come, Follow Me—For Primary*.

Suggested song: "Dear to the Heart of the Shepherd," *Hymns*, no. 221.

Improving Our Teaching

Use stories and examples to teach gospel principles. The Savior often taught about gospel principles by using stories and parables. Think of examples and stories from your own life that can make a gospel principle come alive for your family (see *Teaching in the Savior's Way*, 22).

Where Are the Nine, by Liz Lemon Swindle

Matthew 19–20; Mark 10; Luke 18

"WHAT LACK I YET?"

Read and ponder Matthew 19–20; Mark 10; and Luke 18, paying attention to the promptings you receive. Make note of those promptings, and determine how you will act on them.

RECORD YOUR IMPRESSIONS

If you had the opportunity to ask the Savior a question, what would it be? When a certain rich young man met the Savior for the first time, he asked, "What good thing shall I do, that I may have eternal life?" (Matthew 19:16). The Savior's response showed both appreciation for the good things the young man had already done and loving encouragement to do more. When we ponder the possibility of eternal life, we may similarly wonder if there's more we should be doing. When we ask, in our own way, "What lack I yet?" (Matthew 19:20), the Lord can give us answers that are just as personal as His response to the rich young man. Whatever the Lord asks us to do, acting on His answer will always require that we trust Him more than our own righteousness (see Luke 18:9–14) and that we "receive the kingdom of God as a little child" (Luke 18:17; see also 3 Nephi 9:22).

 Ideas for Personal Scripture Study

MATTHEW 19:3–9; MARK 10:2–12

Marriage between a man and a woman is ordained of God.

This interchange between the Savior and the Pharisees is one of the few recorded instances in which the Savior taught specifically about marriage. After reading Matthew 19:3–9 and Mark 10:2–12, make a list of several statements that you feel summarize the Lord's views on marriage. Then study some of the resources found in "Marriage" (Gospel Topics, topics. ChurchofJesusChrist.org), and add more statements to your list. How does your knowledge of the Father's plan of salvation affect the way you think and feel about marriage?

MATTHEW 19:3–9; MARK 10:2–12

Did Jesus teach that divorce is never acceptable or that divorced people should not remarry?

In an address on divorce, President Dallin H. Oaks taught that Heavenly Father intends for the marriage relationship to be eternal. However, God also understands that divorce is sometimes necessary. President Oaks explained that the Lord "permits divorced persons to marry again without the stain of immorality specified in the higher law. Unless a divorced member has committed serious transgressions, he or she can become eligible for a temple recommend under the same worthiness standards that apply to other members" ("Divorce," *Ensign* or *Liahona*, May 2007, 70).

MATTHEW 19:16–22; MARK 10:17–22; LUKE 18:18–23

If I ask the Lord, He will teach me what I need to do to inherit eternal life.

The account of the rich young man can give pause even to the faithful, lifelong disciple. As you read Mark 10:17–22, what evidence do you find of the young man's faithfulness and sincerity? How did the Lord feel toward this young man?

This account may prompt you to ask, "What lack I yet?" (Matthew 19:20). How does the Lord help us make up for what we lack? (see Ether 12:27). What can we do to prepare ourselves to accept His correction and help as we seek to improve?

See also Larry R. Lawrence, "What Lack I Yet?," *Ensign* or *Liahona*, Nov. 2015, 33–35; S. Mark Palmer, "Then Jesus Beholding Him Loved Him," *Ensign* or *Liahona*, May 2017, 114–16.

MATTHEW 20:1–16

Everyone can receive the blessing of eternal life, no matter when they accept the gospel.

Can you relate to the experience of any of the laborers in the vineyard? What lessons do you find for yourself in this passage? Elder Jeffrey R. Holland's message "The Laborers in the Vineyard" (*Ensign* or *Liahona*, May 2012, 31–33) might help you see new ways to apply this parable. What additional promptings does the Spirit give to you?

The Repentant Publican and the Self-Righteous Pharisee in the Temple, by Frank Adams

I should trust God's mercy, not my own righteousness.

How would you summarize the differences between the two prayers in this parable? Ponder what you feel you should do to be more like the publican in this story and less like the Pharisee.

See also Philippians 4:11–13; Alma 31:12–23; 32:12–16.

 # Ideas for Family Scripture Study and Home Evening

Mark 10:13–16; Luke 18:15–17. To help family members ponder the account in these verses, you could sing together a related song, such as "I Think When I Read That Sweet Story" (*Children's Songbook*, 56). What might it have been like to be among the children Jesus blessed? What might it mean to "receive the kingdom of God as a little child"? (Mark 10:15).

Mark 10:23–27. What is the difference between *having* riches and *trusting in* riches? (see Mark 10:23–24). As you read verse 27, you may want to point out the Joseph Smith Translation: "With men *that trust in riches,* it is impossible; but not *impossible with men who trust in God and leave all for my sake,* for with *such* all *these* things are possible" (Joseph Smith Translation, Mark 10:26 [in Mark 10:27, footnote *a*]). As a family, how are we showing that we trust God more than material things?

Matthew 20:1–16. To illustrate the principles in Matthew 20:1–16, you might set up a simple competition, such as a short race. After everyone has completed the competition, award everyone the same prize, starting with the person who finished last and ending with the person who finished first. What does this teach us about who receives the blessings of eternal life in Heavenly Father's plan?

Matthew 20:25–28; Mark 10:42–45. What is the meaning of the phrase "whosoever will be chief among you, let him be your servant"? (Matthew 20:27). How did Jesus Christ exemplify this principle? How can we follow His example in our family, our ward or branch, and our neighborhood?

Luke 18:1–14. What do we learn about prayer from the two parables in these verses?

For more ideas for teaching children, see this week's outline in *Come, Follow Me—For Primary.*

Suggested song: "Dearest Children, God Is Near You," *Hymns,* no. 96.

Improving Personal Study

Find a time that works for you. It is often easiest to learn when you can study the scriptures without being interrupted. Find a time that works for you, and do your best to consistently study at that time each day.

Christ and the Rich Young Ruler, by Heinrich Hofmann

Matthew 21–23; Mark 11; Luke 19–20; John 12

"BEHOLD, THY KING COMETH"

Before reading the ideas in this outline, read Matthew 21–23; Mark 11; Luke 19–20; and John 12. Record impressions that you could share with your family or in your Church classes.

RECORD YOUR IMPRESSIONS

The Savior was hungry after traveling from Bethany to Jerusalem, and a fig tree in the distance looked like a source of food. But as Jesus approached the tree, He found that it bore no fruit (see Matthew 21:17–20; Mark 11:12–14, 20). In a way, the fig tree was like the hypocritical religious leaders in Jerusalem: their empty teachings and outward demonstrations of holiness gave no spiritual nourishment. The Pharisees and scribes appeared to keep many commandments yet missed the two greatest commandments: to love God and to love thy neighbor as thyself (see Matthew 22:34–40; 23:23).

In contrast, many people had begun to recognize good fruit in Jesus's teachings. When He arrived at Jerusalem, they welcomed Him with branches cut from trees to pave His path, rejoicing that at long last, as ancient prophecy said, "Thy King cometh" (Zechariah 9:9). As you read this week, think about the fruits of the Savior's teachings and atoning sacrifice in your life and how you can bring "forth much fruit" (John 12:24).

 ## Ideas for Personal Scripture Study

LUKE 19:1–10

The Lord judges not by the outward appearance but by the desires of the heart.

In Jesus's day, many people assumed that the publicans, or tax collectors, were dishonest and stole from the people. So because Zacchaeus, the chief publican, was wealthy, he may have been even more suspect. But Jesus looked on Zacchaeus's heart. What does Luke 19:1–10 reveal about Zacchaeus's heart? You might make note of the words in these verses that describe what Zacchaeus did to show his devotion to the Savior. What are the desires of your heart? What are you doing to seek the Savior, as Zacchaeus did?

See also Doctrine and Covenants 137:9.

MATTHEW 23; LUKE 20:45–47

Jesus condemns hypocrisy.

The Savior's interaction with the scribes and Pharisees forms an interesting contrast to his interaction with Zacchaeus. As President Dieter F. Uchtdorf explained, "[Jesus] rose up in righteous anger against hypocrites like the scribes, Pharisees, and Sadducees—those who tried to appear righteous in order to win the praise, influence, and wealth of the world, all the while oppressing the people they should have been blessing" ("On Being Genuine," *Ensign* or *Liahona*, May 2015, 81).

In Matthew 23, the Savior used several metaphors to describe hypocrisy. Consider marking or listing these metaphors and noting what they teach about hypocrisy. What is the difference between hypocrisy and the human weaknesses we all deal with as we try to live the gospel? What are you inspired to do differently because of the Savior's teachings?

See also Bible Dictionary, "Hypocrite."

MATTHEW 21:1–11; MARK 11:1–11; LUKE 19:29–44; JOHN 12:1–8, 12–16

Jesus Christ is my King.

When Jesus arrived at Jerusalem just days before He accomplished His Atonement, those who recognized Him as their King showed their devotion by anointing Him, putting clothes and palm branches along His path into Jerusalem, and shouting praises. Consider how the following resources can deepen your understanding of these events, which began the last week of the Savior's life.

- An ancient example of anointing a king: 2 Kings 9:1–6, 13

- An ancient prophecy of the triumphal entry: Zechariah 9:9

- The meaning of the word *hosanna*: "Hosanna" in Guide to the Scriptures (scriptures .ChurchofJesusChrist.org)

- Prophecies about how the Savior will come again: Revelation 7:9–12

How can you honor and receive the Savior as your Lord and King?

See also Gerrit W. Gong, "Hosanna and Hallelujah—The Living Jesus Christ: The Heart of Restoration and Easter," *Ensign* or *Liahona*, May 2020, 52–55; "The Lord's Triumphal Entry into Jerusalem" (video), ChurchofJesusChrist.org.

MATTHEW 22:34–40

The two great commandments are to love God and love others as myself.

If you ever feel overwhelmed as you strive to follow Jesus Christ, the Savior's words to the lawyer in Matthew 22 can help you simplify and focus your discipleship. Here's one way to do this: Make a list of several of the Lord's commandments. How does each item on your list connect to the two great commandments? How would focusing on the two great commandments help you keep the others?

Ideas for Family Scripture Study and Home Evening

Matthew 21:12–14. How do Jesus's words and actions in Matthew 21:12–14 show how He felt about the temple? How do we show how we feel about the temple? What can we "cast out" (verse 12) of our lives to make our home more like the temple? Consider singing a song about the temple, such as "I Love to See the Temple" (*Children's Songbook*, 95).

Matthew 21:28–32. What lessons from the parable of the man with two sons might help your family? For instance, you could use the story to discuss the importance of sincere obedience and repentance. Perhaps your family could write a script to dramatize the parable and take turns acting out different roles.

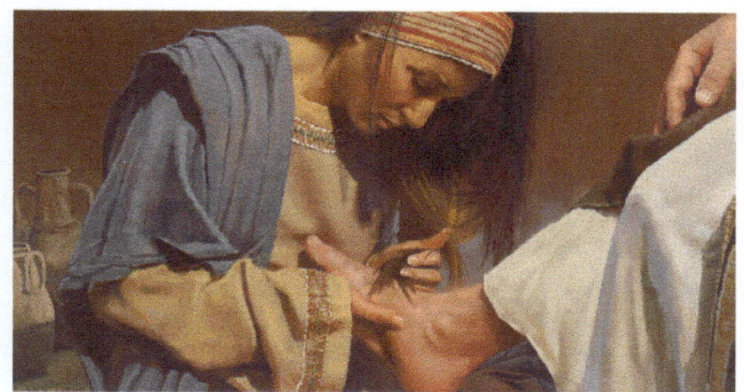
Washing Jesus's Feet, by Brian Call

Matthew 22:15–22; Luke 20:21–26. Children might enjoy making pretend coins with Jesus's "image and superscription" on them. They could write on the backs of the coins some of the "things that are God's" (Matthew 22:21) that we can give Him. You might also talk about what it means to have the Savior's "image and superscription" on *us* (Matthew 22:20; see also Mosiah 5:8; Alma 5:14).

John 12:1–8. How did Mary show her love for the Savior? How do we show our love for Him?

John 12:42–43. What social consequences sometimes discourage us from expressing or defending our belief in Christ? For examples of people who would not give in to social pressure, see Daniel 1:3–20; 3; 6; John 7:45–53; 9:1–38; and Mosiah 17:1–4. How can we show respect to others as they express or defend their religious beliefs?

For more ideas for teaching children, see this week's outline in *Come, Follow Me—For Primary.*

Suggested song: "Rejoice, the Lord Is King!," *Hymns,* no. 66.

Improving Our Teaching

Use art to engage family members. "The *Gospel Art Book* and the Gospel Media Library on ChurchofJesusChrist.org contain many images and videos that can help [your family] visualize concepts or events" (*Teaching in the Savior's Way,* 22).

Triumphal Entry, by Walter Rane

Joseph Smith—Matthew 1; Matthew 24–25; Mark 12–13; Luke 21

"THE SON OF MAN SHALL COME"

As you read Joseph Smith—Matthew 1; Matthew 24–25; Mark 12–13; and Luke 21, you might ask, "What messages do these chapters have for me? for my family? for my calling?"

RECORD YOUR IMPRESSIONS

Jesus's disciples must have found His prophecy startling: the mighty temple of Jerusalem, the spiritual and cultural center of the Jewish people, would be destroyed so utterly that "there [would] not be left . . . one stone upon another." Naturally the disciples wanted to know more. "When shall these things be?" they asked. "And what is the sign of thy coming?" (Joseph Smith—Matthew 1:2–4). The Savior's answers revealed that the great destruction coming to Jerusalem—a prophecy fulfilled in AD 70—would be relatively small compared to the signs of His coming in the last days. Things that seem even more stable than the temple in Jerusalem will prove to be temporary—the sun, the moon, the stars, the nations, and the sea. Even "the powers of heaven shall be shaken" (Joseph Smith—Matthew 1:33). If we are spiritually aware, this commotion can teach us to put our trust in something truly permanent. As Jesus promised, "Heaven and earth shall pass away; yet my words shall not pass away. . . . And whoso treasureth up my word, shall not be deceived" (Joseph Smith—Matthew 1:35, 37).

 ## Ideas for Personal Scripture Study

What is Joseph Smith—Matthew?

Joseph Smith—Matthew, located in the Pearl of Great Price, is the Joseph Smith Translation of the last verse of Matthew 23 and all of Matthew 24. Joseph Smith's inspired revisions restore precious truths that had been lost. Verses 12–21 refer to the destruction of Jerusalem anciently; verses 21–55 contain prophecies about the last days.

JOSEPH SMITH—MATTHEW 1:21–37; MARK 13:21–37; LUKE 21:25–38

Prophecies about the Savior's Second Coming can help me face the future with faith.

It can be unsettling to read about the events leading up to the Second Coming of Jesus Christ. But when Jesus prophesied of these events, He told His disciples to "be not troubled" (Joseph Smith—Matthew 1:23). How can you "be not troubled" as you hear about earthquakes, wars, deceptions, and famines? Think about this question as you read these verses. Mark or note any reassuring counsel you find.

See also Gospel Topics, "Second Coming of Jesus Christ," topics.ChurchofJesusChrist.org.

JOSEPH SMITH—MATTHEW 1:26–27, 38–55; MATTHEW 25:1–13; LUKE 21:29–36

I must always be ready for the Savior's Second Coming.

God has not revealed "the day nor the hour wherein the Son of man cometh" (Matthew 25:13). But He does not want that day to come upon us "unawares" (Luke 21:34), so He has given us counsel about how to prepare.

As you read these verses, identify the parables and other comparisons the Savior used to teach us to always be prepared for His Second Coming. What do you learn from them? What are you inspired to do?

You might also consider how the Savior wants you to help prepare the world for His Second Coming. What do you feel it means to be ready to receive the Savior when He comes? Elder D. Todd Christofferson's message "Preparing for the Lord's Return" (*Ensign* or *Liahona*, May 2019, 81–84) could help you ponder this.

See also Russell M. Nelson, "Embrace the Future with Faith," *Ensign* or *Liahona*, Nov. 2020, 73–76.

MATTHEW 25:14–30

Heavenly Father expects me to use His gifts wisely.

In the Savior's parable, a "talent" referred to money. But the parable of the talents can prompt us to ponder how we are using any of our blessings, not just money. After reading this parable, you might make a list of some of the blessings and responsibilities that Heavenly Father has entrusted to you. What does He expect you to do with these blessings? How can you use these gifts more wisely?

MATTHEW 25:31–46

When I serve others, I am serving God.

If you wonder how the Lord will judge your life, read the parable of the sheep and the goats. Why do you think caring for those in need would help prepare you to "inherit the kingdom" of God?

How is this parable similar to the other two in Matthew 25? What messages do the three have in common?

See also Mosiah 2:17; 5:13.

 ## Ideas for Family Scripture Study and Home Evening

Joseph Smith—Matthew. To help your family explore this chapter, invite them to look for the Savior's teachings about how we can prepare for His Second Coming (see, for example, verses 22–23, 29–30, 37, 46–48). What can we do to follow this counsel? Your family might enjoy singing "When He Comes Again" (*Children's Songbook*, 82–83) and drawing pictures of what they imagine the Savior's Second Coming will be like.

Joseph Smith—Matthew 1:22, 37. What does it mean to treasure up the word of God? How can we do this personally and as a family? How will doing so help us avoid being deceived?

Matthew 25:1–13. You could use the picture of the ten virgins that accompanies this outline to discuss Matthew 25:1–13. What details do we see in the picture that are described in these verses?

Widow's Mite, by Sandra Rast

You might cut paper in the shape of drops of oil and hide the drops around your home. You could attach the drops to objects like the scriptures or a picture of the temple. When family members find the drops, you could discuss how these things help us prepare for the Second Coming.

Mark 12:38–44; Luke 21:1–4. What do these verses teach about how the Savior views our offerings? Show your family how to pay tithing and fast offerings to the Lord. How do these offerings help build God's kingdom? What are some other ways we can offer "all that [we have]" to the Lord? (Mark 12:44).

For more ideas for teaching children, see this week's outline in *Come, Follow Me—For Primary*.

Suggested song: "When He Comes Again," *Children's Songbook*, 82–83.

Improving Personal Study

Prepare your surroundings. "Our surroundings can profoundly affect our ability to learn and feel truth" (*Teaching in the Savior's Way*, 15). Try to find a place to study the scriptures that will invite the influence of the Holy Ghost. Uplifting music and pictures can also invite the Spirit.

Five of Them Were Wise, by Walter Rane

Matthew 26; Mark 14; John 13

"IN REMEMBRANCE"

As you read about the events described in Matthew 26; Mark 14; and John 13, pay attention to any impressions you receive, especially those impressions that deepen your faith in Jesus Christ and your commitment to Him.

RECORD YOUR IMPRESSIONS

The day before He died, Jesus gave His disciples something to remember Him by. He "took bread, and blessed it, and brake it, and gave it to the disciples, and said, Take, eat; this is my body. And he took the cup, and gave thanks, and gave it to them, saying, Drink ye all of it; for this is my blood" (Matthew 26:26–28).

That happened about 2,000 years ago, in a place most of us will never see, in a language few of us can understand. But now, every Sunday in our own meeting places, priesthood holders, authorized to act in the name of Jesus Christ, do what He once did. They take bread and water, bless it, and give it to each of us, His disciples. It's a simple act—can there be anything simpler, more fundamental, than eating bread and drinking water? But that bread and water are sacred to us because they help us remember Him. They're our way of saying, "I'll never forget Him"—not just, "I'll never forget what I've read about His teachings and His life." Rather, we are saying, "I'll never forget what He did for me." "I'll never forget how He rescued me when I cried out for help." And "I'll never forget His commitment to me and my commitment to Him—the covenant we have made."

 Ideas for Personal Scripture Study

MATTHEW 26:6–13; MARK 14:3–9

"She is come . . . to anoint my body to the burying."

With a humble act of worship, the woman described in these verses showed that she knew who Jesus was and what He was about to do (see Matthew 26:12). Why do you think her actions were so meaningful to the Savior? (see verse 13). What impresses you about the woman and her faith? Ponder how you can follow her example.

See also John 12:1–8.

MATTHEW 26:20–22; MARK 14:17–19

"Lord, is it I?"

What do you learn about the disciples from their question to the Lord in these verses? Why do you think they asked it? Consider how you might ask the Lord, "Is it I?"

See also Dieter F. Uchtdorf, "Lord, Is It I?," *Ensign* or *Liahona*, Nov. 2014, 56–59.

MATTHEW 26:26–29; MARK 14:22–25

The sacrament is an opportunity to remember the Savior.

When the Savior introduced the sacrament to His disciples, what thoughts and feelings do you imagine they would have had? Think about this as you read about their experience in Matthew 26:26–29 and Mark 14:22–25. Why do you think Jesus chose this way for us to remember Him? You might also ponder experiences you have had during the sacrament. Is there anything you could do to make your experience more sacred and meaningful?

After reading and pondering these verses, you might write down some things you feel inspired to remember about the Savior. You could review these things the next time you take the sacrament. You could also review them at other times, as a way to "always remember him" (Moroni 4:3).

See also Luke 22:7–39; 3 Nephi 18:1–13; Doctrine and Covenants 20:76–79; Gospel Topics, "Sacrament," topics.ChurchofJesusChrist.org; "Always Remember Him" (video), ChurchofJesusChrist.org.

JOHN 13:1–17

The Savior is our example of humbly serving others.

In Jesus's time, washing another person's feet was a task for servants, not leaders. But Jesus wanted His disciples to think differently about what it means to lead and to serve. What messages do you find in the Savior's words and actions in John 13:1–17? In your culture, washing others' feet may not be a customary way to serve. But consider what you can do to follow the Savior's example of humble service.

It might also be interesting to notice the things that Jesus knew and felt during this sacred time with His Apostles (see verses 1 and 3). What do these insights help you understand about the Savior?

See also Luke 22:24–27.

My love for others is a sign that I am a true disciple of Jesus Christ.

Earlier, Jesus had given a commandment to "love thy neighbour as thyself" (Matthew 22:39). Now He gave "a new commandment." What do you think it means to love others as Jesus loves you? (see John 13:34).

You might also ponder how other people know that you are a disciple of Jesus Christ. How can you make sure that love is your defining characteristic as a Christian?

 # Ideas for Family Scripture Study and Home Evening

Matthew 26:26–29; Mark 14:22–25. What is your family's experience like during the sacrament each week? Reading about the first sacrament could inspire a discussion about the importance of the sacrament and ways to improve your experience. Consider displaying the picture Passing the Sacrament (*Gospel Art Book*, no. 108) and sharing ideas about what you can do before, during, and after the sacrament.

The sacrament helps us remember Jesus Christ.

Matthew 26:30. Consider singing a hymn, as Jesus and His Apostles did—perhaps a sacrament hymn. How might singing a hymn have been a blessing to Jesus and His Apostles at that time? How are hymns a blessing to us?

John 13:1–17. You may want to show your family the picture at the end of this outline as you read these verses. What truths did the Savior teach by His actions? What details in the picture help us understand these truths? Perhaps family members could share how living by these truths has brought them happiness (see John 13:17).

John 13:34–35. After reading these verses, you might talk together about how other people know that you are disciples of Jesus Christ. How does the Savior want His followers to be known? You could ask family members to talk about people whose love for others shows that they are true disciples of Jesus Christ. You might also discuss ways you could show more love as a family.

For more ideas for teaching children, see this week's outline in *Come, Follow Me—For Primary*.

Suggested song: "Love One Another," *Children's Songbook*, 136.

Improving Personal Study

Ponder. The scriptures have spiritual meanings that we may miss if we read too casually, as we would other reading material. Don't be in a hurry to finish a chapter. Take time to think deeply about what you are reading.

Greatest in the Kingdom, by J. Kirk Richards

John 14–17

"CONTINUE YE IN MY LOVE"

As you read the Savior's teachings in John 14–17, the Holy Ghost will help you identify messages for you. Record the impressions you receive.

RECORD YOUR IMPRESSIONS ____

____

____

Today we call it the "Last Supper," but we don't know if Jesus's disciples fully realized, when they gathered for the annual Passover feast, that this would be their last meal with their Master before His death. Jesus, however, "knew that his hour was come" (John 13:1). He would soon face the suffering of Gethsemane, the betrayal and denial of His closest friends, and an agonizing death on the cross. Yet even with all of this looming before Him, Jesus's focus was not on Himself but on His disciples. What would they need to know in the days and years ahead? Jesus's tender teachings in John 14–17 reveal how He feels about His disciples, then and now. Among the many comforting truths He shared was the reassurance that, in one sense, He will never leave us. "If ye keep my commandments," He promised, "ye shall abide in my love" (John 15:10).

 Ideas for Personal Scripture Study

JOHN 14–15

I show my love for Jesus Christ by keeping His commandments.

As you read John 14–15, you might note or mark each use of the word *love*. You may notice the word *commandments* repeated frequently in association with the word *love* in these chapters. What do you learn about the relationship between love and commandments from the Savior's teachings? What other words and phrases do you find associated with *love* in these chapters?

Ponder how the Savior's love has influenced you.

See also John 13:34–35; D. Todd Christofferson, "Abide in My Love," *Ensign* or *Liahona*, Nov. 2016, 48–51.

The Last Supper, by Clark Kelley Price

JOHN 14–16

The Holy Ghost helps me fulfill my purpose as a disciple of Jesus Christ.

It must have been heartbreaking for the disciples to hear that their time with the Savior was almost over. They might also have worried about how they would get along without Him. As you read John 14–16, look for what the Savior said to reassure them. In particular, notice what He taught them about the Holy Ghost. What do you learn about the Holy Ghost from the Savior's words in the following verses?

- John 14:16–17, 26 ___________________________
- John 15:26 ___________________________
- John 16:7–11 ___________________________
- John 16:12–15 ___________________________

Why did the disciples need this kind of help from the Holy Ghost? How has the Holy Ghost fulfilled these roles for you? Consider what you can do so that His influence will be stronger in your life.

See also 3 Nephi 19:9; 27:20; Doctrine and Covenants 11:12–14; Moses 6:61; Michelle D. Craig, "Spiritual Capacity," *Ensign* or *Liahona*, Nov. 2019, 19–21.

JOHN 15:1–8

As I abide in Christ, I will bring forth good fruit.

What do you think it means to "abide in [Christ]"? (John 15:4). What is your "fruit" that shows that you are attached to the vine, which represents Jesus Christ?

JOHN 17

Jesus Christ intercedes for His disciples.

Jesus's words recorded in John 17 are known as the Intercessory Prayer. In this prayer, Jesus prayed for His Apostles and "them also which shall believe on [Him] through their word" (John 17:20). That means He was praying for you. What did Jesus request from His Father in behalf of you and all other believers? What does that teach you about His feelings for you?

This prayer also teaches profound, eternal truths. What truths do you find? As you read this chapter, consider recording what you learn about the following:

- Prayer
- The Savior's relationship with His Father
- The Savior's relationship with His disciples
- How disciples are to be different from the world
- Other truths that stand out to you

Heavenly Father and Jesus Christ are perfectly united.

In His prayer in John 17, Jesus emphasized His unity with the Father. In what ways are the Father and the Son "one"? (John 17:11, 21–23). Note that the Savior prayed that His disciples may be one "even as"—or in the same way that—He and His Father are one (John 17:22). What does that mean for you? Think about your relationships—for example, with your spouse or other family members, with ward members, and with fellow Christians. How can you work toward the kind of unity that Jesus has with the Father?

See also Quentin L. Cook, "Hearts Knit in Righteousness and Unity," *Ensign* or *Liahona*, Nov. 2020, 18–21; Sharon Eubank, "By Union of Feeling We Obtain Power with God," *Ensign* or *Liahona*, Nov. 2020, 55–57.

Ideas for Family Scripture Study and Home Evening

John 14:5–6. Family members may enjoy taking turns leading your family on a walk along a path. How is Jesus "the way"? Where does He lead us?

John 14:26–27. How is Jesus's peace different from the kind "the world giveth"? Family members could share ways they have found peace and comfort through the Holy Ghost.

John 15:1–8. It might be fun to read these verses outside next to a vine, a tree, or another plant. What happens to a branch when it is removed from the plant? You could talk about how we are like branches and what it means to "abide" in the Savior and "bear fruit."

John 15:17–27; 16:1–7. Why do you think Jesus Christ warned His disciples of persecution? How are disciples of Christ persecuted today? How can the Savior's counsel in these verses help us when we face persecution?

John 16:33. How has Jesus Christ overcome the world? How has His Atonement brought us peace and good cheer? (see also Doctrine and Covenants 68:6).

John 17:21–23. What would help your family learn how to be more united like Jesus Christ and Heavenly Father? Maybe you could talk about a favorite sports team and how they work together toward a common goal. Or you could listen to a choir or orchestra and discuss how the musicians unite to create beautiful music.

For more ideas for teaching children, see this week's outline in *Come, Follow Me—For Primary*.

Suggested song: "The Holy Ghost," *Children's Songbook*, 105.

Improving Our Teaching

Use audio recordings. As you teach your family the scriptures, consider listening to the audio version of the scriptures, found on ChurchofJesusChrist.org or in the Gospel Library app. Listening to John 14–17 can be particularly powerful because these chapters contain so many of the Savior's words.

Jesus taught, "I am the vine, ye are the branches" (John 15:5).

Gethsemane Grove, by Derek Hegsted

Luke 22; John 18

"NOT MY WILL, BUT THINE, BE DONE"

Take your time reading Luke 22 and John 18 this week. Ponder and pray about what you read. Doing this can give the Spirit opportunity to bear witness to your heart that the scriptures are true.

RECORD YOUR IMPRESSIONS

There were only three mortal witnesses to Jesus Christ's suffering in the Garden of Gethsemane—and they slept through much of it. In that garden and later on the cross, Jesus took upon Himself the sins, pains, and sufferings of every person who ever lived, although almost no one alive at that time knew what was happening. Eternity's most important events often pass without much worldly attention. But God the Father knew. He heard the pleading of His faithful Son: "Father, if thou be willing, remove this cup from me: nevertheless not my will, but thine, be done. And there appeared an angel unto him from heaven, strengthening him" (Luke 22:42–43). While we were not there to witness this act of selflessness and submission, we *are* witnesses of the Atonement of Jesus Christ. Every time we repent and receive forgiveness of our sins, every time we feel the Savior's strengthening power, we can testify of the reality of what happened in the Garden of Gethsemane.

 Ideas for Personal Scripture Study

LUKE 22:31–34, 54–62; JOHN 18:17–27

Conversion is an ongoing process.

Think about the experiences Peter had with the Savior—the miracles he witnessed and the doctrine he learned. Why then would the Savior say to Peter, "*When* thou art converted, strengthen thy brethren"? (Luke 22:32; italics added). As you ponder this, it might help to consider what Elder David A. Bednar taught about the difference between having a testimony and being truly converted (see "Converted unto the Lord," *Ensign* or *Liahona*, Nov. 2012, 106–9).

As you read about Peter's experiences in Luke 22:31–34, 54–62 (see also John 18:17–27), think about your own conversion. Have you ever felt so committed that, like Peter, you were "ready to go with [the Savior], both into prison, and to death"? (Luke 22:33). Why do those feelings sometimes fade? There are daily opportunities to either deny or witness of the Savior; what will you do to be a daily witness of Him? What other lessons do you learn from Peter's experience?

As you continue reading the New Testament, watch for evidence of Peter's ongoing conversion. Also note ways he accepted the Lord's charge to "strengthen thy brethren" (Luke 22:32; see Acts 3–4).

See also Mark 14:27–31.

LUKE 22:39–46

The Savior suffered for me in Gethsemane.

President Russell M. Nelson invited us to "invest time in learning about the Savior and His atoning sacrifice" ("Drawing the Power of Jesus Christ into Our Lives," *Ensign* or *Liahona*, May 2017, 40).

Consider what you will do to accept President Nelson's invitation. You might start by prayerfully pondering the Savior's suffering in Gethsemane, as described in these verses, and writing impressions and questions that come to mind.

For an even deeper study of the Savior and His Atonement, try searching other scriptures for answers to questions like these:

- Why was the Savior's Atonement necessary? (See 2 Nephi 2:5–10, 17–26; 9:5–26; Alma 34:8–16; 42:9–26.)

- What did the Savior experience as He suffered? (See Isaiah 53:3–5; Mosiah 3:7; Alma 7:11–13; Doctrine and Covenants 19:16–19.)

- How does Christ's suffering affect my life? (See John 10:10–11; Hebrews 4:14–16; 1 John 1:7; Alma 34:31; Moroni 10:32–33; Dallin H. Oaks, "Strengthened by the Atonement of Jesus Christ," *Ensign* or *Liahona*, Nov. 2015, 61–64.)

- Other questions I have:

____

____

As you learn about what happened in Gethsemane, it might be interesting to know that Gethsemane was a garden of olive trees and included an olive press, used to crush olives and extract oil used for lighting and food as well as healing (see Luke 10:34). How might the process of extracting olive oil symbolize what the Savior did for us in Gethsemane? For some ideas, see Elder D. Todd Christofferson's message "Abide in My Love" (*Ensign* or *Liahona*, Nov. 2016, 50–51).

See also Matthew 26:36–46; Mark 14:32–42.

JOHN 18:28–38

The Savior's "kingdom is not of this world."

As a political leader, Pontius Pilate was familiar with the power and kingdoms of this world. But Jesus spoke of a much different kind of kingdom. Thinking back on what you've read about the Savior's life, what evidence do you see that His "kingdom is not of this world"? (John 18:36). Why is it important for you to know this? What else stands out to you about Jesus's words to Pilate?

Ideas for Family Scripture Study and Home Evening

Luke 22:31–32. How might Peter have felt to know that Jesus had prayed for him and his faith? Who can we pray for, "that [their] faith fail not"? (verse 32).

Luke 22:39–46. Learning about the Savior's suffering in Gethsemane can be a sacred experience for your family. Consider what you can do to create a reverent and worshipful spirit as you study Luke 22:39–46. You might play or sing together some of your family's favorite hymns or children's songs about the Savior. You could look at related artwork or watch a video like "The Savior Suffers in Gethsemane" (ChurchofJesusChrist.org). As you read the verses, family members could share passages that are especially meaningful to them—perhaps a passage that helps them feel the Savior's love (see also Matthew 26:36–46; Mark 14:32–42). You might also invite them to share their testimonies of Jesus Christ and His Atonement.

Luke 22:42. Family members could share experiences when they learned to say, "Not my will, but thine, be done."

Luke 22:50–51; John 18:10–11. What do we learn about Jesus from these verses?

Suffer Ye Thus Far, by Walter Rane

John 18:37–38. How would we answer Pilate's question "What is truth?" (verse 38). For some ideas, see John 8:32; Doctrine and Covenants 84:45; 93:23–28; and "Oh Say, What Is Truth?," *Hymns,* no. 272.

For more ideas for teaching children, see this week's outline in *Come, Follow Me—For Primary.*

Suggested song: "I Stand All Amazed," *Hymns,* no. 193.

Improving Personal Study

Study the words of latter-day prophets and apostles. Read what latter-day prophets and apostles have taught about the truths you find in the scriptures. For instance, in the most recent general conference issue of the *Liahona,* you could search the topic index for "Atonement" (see *Teaching in the Savior's Way,* 21).

Not My Will, but Thine, by Walter Rane

Ecce Homo, by Antonio Ciseri

Matthew 27; Mark 15; Luke 23; John 19

"IT IS FINISHED"

Matthew 27; Mark 15; Luke 23; and John 19 include descriptions of the final hours of the Savior's mortal life. Seek to feel His love for you as you study about His sacrifice and death.

RECORD YOUR IMPRESSIONS

In every word and deed, Jesus Christ exemplified pure love—what the Apostle Paul called charity (see 1 Corinthians 13). At no time was this more evident than during the final hours of the Savior's mortal life. His dignified silence in the face of false accusations demonstrated that He "is not easily provoked" (1 Corinthians 13:5). His willingness to submit to scourging, mocking, and crucifixion—while restraining His power to end His torments—showed that He "suffereth long" and "beareth all things" (1 Corinthians 13:4, 7). His compassion toward His mother and His mercy toward His crucifiers—even during His own incomparable suffering—revealed that He "seeketh not [His] own" (1 Corinthians 13:5). In His final moments on earth, Jesus was doing what He had done throughout His mortal ministry—teaching us by showing us. Indeed, charity is "the pure love of Christ" (Moroni 7:47).

Ideas for Personal Scripture Study

MATTHEW 27; MARK 15; LUKE 23; JOHN 19

Jesus Christ's willingness to suffer shows His love for the Father and for all of us.

Although the Savior had power to call down "legions of angels" (Matthew 26:53), He voluntarily chose to endure unjust trials, cruel mocking, and unimaginable physical pain. Why did He do it? "Because of his loving kindness," Nephi testified, "and his long-suffering towards the children of men" (1 Nephi 19:9).

"And he bearing his cross went forth into . . . Golgotha" (John 19:17).

You might begin your study of the Savior's final hours by reading 1 Nephi 19:9. Where in Matthew 27; Mark 15; Luke 23; and John 19 do you find examples of each thing that Nephi said Jesus would suffer?

"[They] judge him to be a thing of naught"____

"They scourge him"____

"They smite him"____

"They spit upon him"____

Which passages help you feel the Savior's "loving kindness" toward you? What other thoughts and feelings do you have as you read these accounts? Consider writing them down or sharing them with someone.

See also "Jesus Is Condemned before Pilate" and "Jesus Is Scourged and Crucified" (videos), ChurchofJesusChrist.org.

MATTHEW 27:27–49, 54; MARK 15:16–32; LUKE 23:11, 35–39; JOHN 19:1–5

Mocking cannot change the truth.

While Jesus had endured mocking throughout His ministry, it grew more intense during His scourging and Crucifixion. But this mocking could not change the truth: Jesus is the Son of God. As you read about the humiliation Jesus endured, think about the opposition and mocking His work faces today. What insights do you gain about enduring opposition? What impresses you about the centurion's words in Matthew 27:54?

MATTHEW 27:46; MARK 15:34

Jesus Christ suffered alone so I don't have to.

During one of His most poignant moments on the cross, Jesus, who had always relied on His Heavenly Father, suddenly felt forsaken. Reading about this might lead you to think about times when you've felt distant from God. You might ponder how the Savior's sacrifice on the cross makes it possible for you to overcome that distance. As Elder Jeffrey R. Holland testified, "Because Jesus walked such a long, lonely path utterly alone, *we* do not have to do so. . . . Trumpeted from the summit of Calvary is the truth that we will never be left alone nor unaided, even if sometimes we may feel that we are" ("None Were with Him," *Ensign* or *Liahona*, May 2009, 88). Consider how the Savior can help you overcome loneliness as you read the rest of Elder Holland's message.

The Savior is our example of forgiveness.

How do you feel when you read the Savior's words in Luke 23:34? (see the insight provided by the Joseph Smith Translation in footnote *c*). Referring to the Savior's words, President Henry B. Eyring taught: "We must forgive and bear no malice toward those who offend us. The Savior set the example from the cross. . . . We do not know the hearts of those who offend us" ("That We May Be One," *Ensign*, May 1998, 68). How can this verse help you if you have trouble forgiving someone?

 ## Ideas for Family Scripture Study and Home Evening

Matthew 27; Mark 15; Luke 23; John 19. To help your family learn about the events described in these chapters, you could share with them "Chapter 52: The Trials of Jesus" and "Chapter 53: Jesus Is Crucified" (in *New Testament Stories*, 133–38, or the corresponding videos on ChurchofJesusChrist.org). Or you could watch together videos depicting these events: "Jesus Is Condemned before Pilate" and "Jesus Is Scourged and Crucified" (ChurchofJesusChrist.org). You might invite children to retell the stories in their own words. Family members could share how they feel toward the Savior because of what He suffered for us.

Matthew 27:11–26; Mark 15:1–15; Luke 23:12–25; John 19:1–16. Why did Pilate deliver Jesus to be crucified, even though he knew Jesus was innocent? What lessons do we learn from Pilate's experience about standing up for what we know is right? It might be helpful for your family to role-play scenarios that allow them to practice standing up for what is right.

Matthew 27:46; Luke 23:34, 43, 46; John 19:26–28, 30. Perhaps you could assign each family member to read one or more of the statements the Savior made on the cross, found in these verses. Ask them to share what they learn from these statements about the Savior and His mission.

Mark 15:39. How has reading about the Crucifixion strengthened your testimony that Jesus is the "Son of God"?

John 19:25–27. What do we learn from these verses about how we can love and support family members?

For more ideas for teaching children, see this week's outline in *Come, Follow Me—For Primary*.

Suggested hymn: "Upon the Cross of Calvary," *Hymns*, no. 184.

Improving Our Teaching

Emulate the Savior's life. "It is helpful to study the ways the Savior taught—the methods He used and the things He said. But the Savior's power to teach and lift others came from the way He lived and the kind of person He was. The more diligently you strive to *live* like Jesus Christ, the more you will be able to *teach* like Him" (*Teaching in the Savior's Way*, 13).

Christ on the Cross, by Carl Heinrich Bloch

Matthew 28; Mark 16; Luke 24; John 20–21

"HE IS RISEN"

Prayerfully read Matthew 28; Mark 16; Luke 24; and John 20–21, reflecting on the joy you have because of the Resurrection of Christ. Who might be blessed by hearing your testimony of this event?

RECORD YOUR IMPRESSIONS

To many observers, the death of Jesus of Nazareth may have seemed like an ironic end to a remarkable life. Wasn't this the man who raised Lazarus from the dead? Hadn't He withstood the murderous threats from the Pharisees time after time? He had demonstrated power to heal blindness, leprosy, and palsy. The very winds and the seas obeyed Him. And yet here He was, hanging from a cross, declaring, "It is finished" (John 19:30). There may have been some sincere surprise in the mocking words "He saved others; himself he cannot save" (Matthew 27:42). But we know that Jesus's death was not the end of the story. We know that the silence of the tomb was temporary and that Christ's saving work was just beginning. He is found today not "among the dead" but among the living (Luke 24:5). His teachings would not be silenced, for His loyal disciples would preach the gospel in "all nations," trusting His promise that He would be "with [them] alway, even unto the end of the world" (Matthew 28:19–20).

Ideas for Personal Scripture Study

MATTHEW 28; MARK 16; LUKE 24; JOHN 20

Jesus Christ was resurrected.

In these passages, you will read about one of the most important events in the history of humankind: the Resurrection of Jesus Christ. As you read, put yourself in the place of the people who witnessed the events surrounding the Resurrection. What do you learn from their experiences?

How do *you* feel as you read about the Savior's Resurrection? Consider how it has affected you—your outlook on life, your relationships, your faith in Christ, and your faith in other gospel truths.

See also Bible Dictionary, "Resurrection"; Gospel Topics, "Resurrection," topics.Church ofJesusChrist.org.

LUKE 24:13–35

I can invite the Savior to "abide with [me]."

As you read the experience of the two traveling disciples who met the resurrected Savior, look for parallels to your experiences as a follower of Christ. How can you walk with Him today and invite Him to "tarry" a little longer? (Luke 24:29). How do you recognize His presence in your life? In what ways has the Holy Ghost testified of the divinity of Jesus Christ to you?

See also "Abide with Me; 'Tis Eventide," "Abide with Me!," *Hymns*, nos. 165–66.

LUKE 24:36–43; JOHN 20

Resurrection is the permanent reuniting of the spirit with the body.

The accounts of the Resurrection of Jesus Christ can help you understand what it means to be resurrected. For example, what truths do you find in Luke 24:36–43 and John 20 about resurrected bodies? You could also explore other scriptures about resurrection, such as 1 Corinthians 15:35–44; Philippians 3:20–21; 3 Nephi 11:13–15; Doctrine and Covenants 88:27–31; 110:2–3; 130:1, 22.

JOHN 20:19–29

"Blessed are they that have not seen, and yet have believed."

Some people feel like Thomas, who said, "Except I shall see . . . , I will not believe" (John 20:25). In your opinion, why can believing without seeing be a blessing? (see John 20:29). Ponder how you have been blessed for believing in things you could not see. What helps you have faith in the Savior even when you cannot see Him? How can you continue to strengthen your faith in "things which are not seen, which are true"? (see Alma 32:16–21; Ether 12:6). Consider recording in a journal experiences that have helped you believe in Jesus Christ, or share them with someone you know.

JOHN 21:1–17

The Savior invites me to feed His sheep.

It might be interesting to compare the Savior's interaction with His Apostles in John 21 to the first time He commanded them to let down their fishing nets, recorded in Luke 5:1–11. What similarities and differences do you find? What insights about discipleship do you find?

Consider how the Savior's words to Peter in John 21:15–17 might apply to you. Is there anything holding you back from ministering to the Lord's sheep? What would your response be if the Lord asked you, "Lovest thou me?" Ponder how you can show your love for the Lord.

See also 1 Peter 5:2–4, 8; Jeffrey R. Holland, "The First Great Commandment," *Ensign* or *Liahona*, Nov. 2012, 83–85.

 ## Ideas for Family Scripture Study and Home Evening

Luke 24:5–6. President Thomas S. Monson said of Luke 24:5–6, "No words in Christendom mean more to me" ("He Is Risen!," *Ensign* or *Liahona*, May 2010, 89). What do these words mean to you and your family?

Matthew 28; Mark 16; Luke 24; John 20–21. As your family reads these chapters, notice the people who interacted with Jesus in each account. For example, what impresses you about the people who visited the Savior's tomb? What do you learn from the words or actions of the Apostles or the disciples on the road to Emmaus?

Consider singing together "Did Jesus Really Live Again?" (*Children's Songbook*, 64). Talk about someone your family knows who has died, and discuss how the truths in this song bring comfort.

Road to Emmaus, by Wendy Keller

Matthew 28:16–20; Mark 16:14–20; Luke 24:44–53. In these verses, what was Jesus asking His Apostles to do? How can we help accomplish this work? Family members could share experiences when they felt "the Lord working with them" to accomplish His purposes (Mark 16:20).

John 21:15–17. Consider reading these verses while eating together. This could add some meaning to the Savior's words "feed my sheep." Based on what Jesus taught about sheep in the New Testament (see, for example, Matthew 9:35–36; 10:5–6; 25:31–46; Luke 15:4–7; John 10:1–16), why is feeding sheep a good way to describe serving God's children? What does this analogy teach about how Heavenly Father and Jesus feel about us?

For more ideas for teaching children, see this week's outline in *Come, Follow Me—For Primary.*

Suggested song: "Did Jesus Really Live Again?," *Children's Songbook*, 64.

Improving Personal Study

Use music to invite the Spirit and learn doctrine. Listening to or singing hymns such as "He Is Risen!" (*Hymns*, no. 199) can invite the Spirit and help you learn about the Savior's Resurrection.

The Resurrected Christ, by Walter Rane

Acts 1–5

"YE SHALL BE WITNESSES UNTO ME"

As you study Acts 1–5, the Holy Ghost can inspire you to find truths that are relevant for your life. Take note of verses that impress you, and look for opportunities to share what you are learning.

RECORD YOUR IMPRESSIONS

Have you ever wondered what Peter might have been thinking and feeling when he, with the other Apostles, "looked steadfastly toward heaven" as Jesus ascended to His Father? (Acts 1:10). The Church that was founded by the Son of God was now in Peter's care. The task of leading the effort to "teach all nations" now rested on him (Matthew 28:19). But if he felt inadequate or afraid, we don't find any evidence of that in the book of Acts. What we do find are examples of fearless testimony and conversion, miraculous healings, spiritual manifestations, and significant growth for the Church. This was still the Savior's Church, still led by Him. In fact, the book Acts of the Apostles could also be called the Acts of Jesus Christ through His Apostles. Guided by an outpouring of the Spirit, Peter was no longer the unlearned fisherman Jesus found on the shores of the Sea of Galilee. Nor was he the distraught man who only weeks earlier was weeping bitterly because he had denied that he even knew Jesus of Nazareth.

In the book of Acts, you will read powerful declarations about Jesus Christ and His gospel. You will also see how that gospel can change people—including you—into the valiant disciples God knows they can be.

 ## Ideas for Personal Scripture Study

ACTS 1:1–8, 15–26; 2:1–42; 4:1–13, 31–33

Jesus Christ directs His Church through the Holy Ghost.

The book of Acts records the Apostles' efforts to establish the Church of Jesus Christ after the Savior's Ascension. Although Jesus Christ was no longer on the earth, He directed the Church by revelation through the Holy Ghost. Consider how the Holy Ghost guided the new leaders of Christ's Church as you review the following passages: Acts 1:1–8, 15–26; 2:1–42; 4:1–13, 31–33.

As members of Christ's Church today, we each have a responsibility to participate in the work of salvation and exaltation—to live the gospel of Jesus Christ, care for those in need, invite others to come unto Christ, and unite families for eternity (see *General Handbook*, 1.2). What do you learn from these early Apostles about how you can rely on the Holy Ghost to guide your efforts?

See also Bible Dictionary, "Holy Ghost."

ACTS 2:36–47; 3:12–21

The principles and ordinances of the gospel help me come unto Christ.

Have you ever felt "pricked in [your] heart," like the Jews on the day of Pentecost? (Acts 2:37). Maybe you did something you regret, or maybe you simply want to change your life. What should you do when you have these feelings? Peter's counsel to the Jews is found in Acts 2:38. Note how the first principles and ordinances of the gospel (including faith, repentance, baptism, and the gift of the Holy Ghost—or what is sometimes referred to as the doctrine of Christ) affected these converts, as recorded in Acts 2:37–47.

You may already have been baptized and received the gift of the Holy Ghost, so how do you continue to apply the doctrine of Christ? Consider these words from Elder Dale G. Renlund: "We may be perfected by repeatedly . . . exercising faith in [Christ], repenting, partaking of the sacrament to renew the covenants and blessings of baptism, and receiving the Holy Ghost as a constant companion to a greater degree. As we do so, we become more like Christ and are able to endure to the end, with all that that entails" ("Latter-day Saints Keep on Trying," *Ensign* or *Liahona*, May 2015, 56).

ACTS 3:19–21

What are "the times of refreshing" and "the times of restitution of all things"?

"The times of refreshing" refers to the Millennium, when Jesus Christ will return to the earth. "The times of restitution of all things" refers to the Restoration of the gospel, which prepares the world for the Millennium.

ACTS 3; 4:1–31; 5:12–42

Disciples of Jesus Christ are given power to perform miracles in His name.

The lame man was hoping to receive money from those who came to the temple. But the Lord's servants offered him much more. As you read Acts 3; 4:1–31 and 5:12–42, consider how the miracle that followed affected these people:

The lame man

Peter and John

The witnesses at the temple

The high priests and rulers

Other Saints

 ## Ideas for Family Scripture Study and Home Evening

Acts 1:21–26. Reading Acts 1:21–26 can help your family discuss the blessings that come from having Apostles on the earth today. Family members could share how they have gained a witness that today's apostles and prophets are called by God. Why is having this witness important?

Such as I Have I Give Thee, by Walter Rane

Acts 2:37. What could the phrase "pricked in their heart" mean? When have we felt something similar? Why is it important to say "What shall we do?" when we have such feelings?

Acts 3:1–10. Your family might enjoy acting out the account in these verses. Or you could watch the video "Peter and John Heal a Man Crippled Since Birth" (ChurchofJesusChrist .org). How was the man at the temple blessed differently than he was expecting? How have we seen Heavenly Father's blessings come to us in unexpected ways?

Acts 3:12–26; 4:1–21; 5:12–42. What impresses you about the faithfulness of Peter and John? (see also the video "Peter Preaches and Is Arrested" on ChurchofJesusChrist.org). How can we be bold in our testimonies of Jesus Christ? Consider helping younger children practice sharing their testimonies.

Acts 4:31–5:4. How can we help our family, ward, or community become more like what is described in Acts 4:31–37? What does it mean to be "of one heart and of one soul"? In what ways do we sometimes "[keep] back part" of our contribution? Why is doing that like "[lying] unto God"? (Acts 5:2, 4). How does dishonesty affect us spiritually?

For more ideas for teaching children, see this week's outline in *Come, Follow Me—For Primary*.

Suggested hymn: "Let the Holy Spirit Guide," *Hymns*, no. 143.

Improving Our Teaching

Pick a topic. Let family members take turns choosing a topic from Acts 1–5 to study together.

The Ascension, by Harry Anderson

Conversion on the Way to Damascus, by Michelangelo Merisi da Caravaggio

Acts 6–9

"WHAT WILT THOU HAVE ME TO DO?"

Begin by reading Acts 6–9. The suggestions in this outline can help you identify some of the important principles in these chapters, though you may find others in your own study.

RECORD YOUR IMPRESSIONS

If anyone seemed like an unlikely candidate for conversion, it was probably Saul—a Pharisee who had a reputation for persecuting Christians. So when the Lord told a disciple named Ananias to seek out Saul and offer him a blessing, Ananias was understandably hesitant. "Lord," he said, "I have heard by many of this man, how much evil he hath done to thy saints" (Acts 9:13). But the Lord knew Saul's heart and his potential, and He had a mission in mind for Saul: "He is a chosen vessel unto me, to bear my name before the Gentiles, and kings, and the children of Israel" (Acts 9:15). So Ananias obeyed, and when he found this former persecutor, he called him "Brother Saul" (Acts 9:17). If Saul could change so completely and Ananias could welcome him so freely, then should we ever consider anyone an unlikely candidate for change—including ourselves?

 Ideas for Personal Scripture Study

My heart needs to be "right in the sight of God."

A growing church meant a growing need for disciples to serve in the kingdom. According to Acts 6:1–5, what qualities were the Twelve Apostles looking for in those who would serve with them? As you read Acts 6–8, note how these qualities, and others, were demonstrated in people like Stephen and Philip. What was lacking in Simon, and what can we learn from him about being willing to change?

Is there anything you feel inspired to change to ensure that your heart is "right in the sight of God"? (Acts 8:21–22). How might making this change bless you as you serve God?

ACTS 6–7

Resisting the Holy Ghost can lead to rejecting the Savior and His servants.

The Jewish leaders were responsible for preparing the people for the coming of the Messiah. And yet they failed to recognize the Messiah and rejected Him. How did this happen? Part of the answer may be found in Stephen's words: "Ye do always resist the Holy Ghost" (Acts 7:51). What do you think it means to resist the Holy Ghost? Why does resisting the Holy Ghost lead to rejecting the Savior and His servants?

As you read Acts 6–7, look for other messages that Stephen taught the Jews. What attitudes was he warning against? Do you detect any similar attitudes in yourself? What do Stephen's words teach you about the consequences of resisting the Holy Ghost? How can you be more sensitive and responsive to the promptings of the Holy Ghost in your life?

See also "The Martyrdom of Stephen" (video), ChurchofJesusChrist.org.

ACTS 8:26–39

The Holy Ghost will help me guide others to Jesus Christ.

What do you learn about sharing the gospel from the account in Acts 8:26–39? How did the Holy Ghost help Philip? How is sharing the gospel with others like being a guide? (see Acts 8:31).

Elder Ulisses Soares said that this account "is a reminder of the divine mandate we all have to seek to learn and to teach one another the gospel of Jesus Christ. . . . We are sometimes like the Ethiopian—we need the help of a faithful and inspired teacher; and we are sometimes like Philip—we need to teach and strengthen others in their conversion" ("How Can I Understand?," *Ensign* or *Liahona*, May 2019, 6). Consider reading the rest of Elder Soares's message and pondering how the Holy Ghost can help you be a better learner and teacher of the gospel.

ACTS 9

When I submit to the Lord's will, I can become an instrument in His hands.

Saul's conversion seems very sudden; he went quickly from imprisoning Christians to preaching about Christ in the synagogues. As you read his story, ponder why he was so willing to change. (To read Saul's own description of his conversion, see Acts 22:1–16 and 26:9–18. Note that in these accounts, Saul goes by the name of Paul [see Acts 13:9].)

While it's true that Saul's experience is unusual—for most people, conversion is a much longer process—is there anything you can learn from Saul about conversion? What do you learn from the way Ananias and the other disciples reacted to Saul's conversion? What will you do to apply these lessons in your life? You might begin by asking in prayer, as Saul did, "What wilt thou have me to do?"

As you read Acts 9:36–42, consider how Tabitha was an instrument in God's hands. What inspires you about her example?

See also Dieter F. Uchtdorf, "Waiting on the Road to Damascus," *Ensign* or *Liahona*, May 2011, 70–77; "The Road to Damascus" (video), ChurchofJesusChrist.org.

Ideas for Family Scripture Study and Home Evening

Acts 6:8; 7:51–60. Compare the accounts of Stephen in Acts 6:8 and Acts 7:51–60 to the accounts of the Savior in Luke 23:1–46. How did Stephen follow the Savior's example?

Acts 7:51–60. How did the Holy Ghost bless Stephen when he was being persecuted? When have we received strength from the Holy Ghost during difficult times?

Acts 9:5. A *prick* was a sharp spear used to drive animals. Often the animals would kick back when pricked, which would cause the spear to sink even further into the animal's flesh. How might this analogy sometimes apply to us? What can we do to better accept correction from the Lord?

Tabitha Arise, by Sandy Freckleton Gagon

Acts 9:32–43. Consider inviting your family members to draw pictures of the stories in Acts 9:32–43. What do we learn about true discipleship from these stories? How can someone who is "full of good works," as Tabitha was, help others believe in the Lord? (see Acts 9:36; "Chapter 60: Peter Brings Tabitha Back to Life," in *New Testament Stories*, 156–57, or the corresponding video on ChurchofJesusChrist.org).

For more ideas for teaching children, see this week's outline in *Come, Follow Me—For Primary.*

Suggested hymn: "I'll Go Where You Want Me to Go," *Hymns,* no. 270.

Improving Personal Study

Liken the scriptures to your life. As you read, consider how the stories and teachings in the scriptures apply in your life. For example, what opportunities do you have to serve others, as Tabitha did in Acts 9:36–39?

"And they stoned Stephen, and he, calling upon God, said, Lord Jesus, receive my spirit" (Joseph Smith Translation, Acts 7:59 [in Acts 7:59, footnote *c*]).

Acts 10–15

"THE WORD OF GOD GREW AND MULTIPLIED"

Read Acts 10–15 carefully, allowing time for the Spirit to prompt you with thoughts and feelings. What is there for you to learn in these chapters?

RECORD YOUR IMPRESSIONS____

During His mortal ministry, Jesus Christ often challenged people's long-held traditions and beliefs. This didn't stop after He ascended into heaven, as He continued to guide His Church by revelation. For example, during Jesus's life His disciples preached the gospel only to fellow Jews. But soon after the Savior died and Peter became the leader of the Church on earth, Jesus Christ revealed to Peter that the time was right for the gospel to be preached to non-Jews. The idea of sharing the gospel with Gentiles doesn't seem surprising today, so what's the lesson in this account for us? Perhaps one lesson is that in both the ancient and modern Church, a loving Savior guides His chosen leaders (see Amos 3:7; Doctrine and Covenants 1:38). Continuing revelation is a vital sign of the true and living Church of Jesus Christ. Like Peter, we must be willing to accept continuing revelation and live "by every word of God" (Luke 4:4), including "all that [He] has revealed, all that He does now reveal," and the "many great and important things" He will yet reveal "pertaining to the Kingdom of God" (Articles of Faith 1:9).

Ideas for Personal Scripture Study

ACTS 10

"God is no respecter of persons."

For generations, the Jews had believed that being of "the seed of Abraham," or a literal descendant of Abraham, meant that a person was accepted and chosen by God (see Luke 3:8).

They considered anyone else an "unclean" Gentile who was not accepted by God. In Acts 10, what did the Lord teach Peter about who "is accepted with him"? (Acts 10:35). What evidence do you find in this chapter that Cornelius's life was acceptable to the Lord? Ponder what is meant by the statement "God is no respecter of persons" (verse 34; see also 1 Nephi 17:35). Why is it important to you to know this truth?

Like the Jews who looked down on those who were not of the seed of Abraham, do you ever catch yourself making unkind or uninformed assumptions about someone who is different from you? How can you overcome this tendency? It might be interesting to try a simple activity for the next few days: Whenever you interact with someone, try to think to yourself, "This person is a child of God." As you do this, what changes do you notice in the way you think about and interact with others?

See also 1 Samuel 16:7; 2 Nephi 26:13, 33; Russell M. Nelson, "Let God Prevail," *Ensign* or *Liahona*, Nov. 2020, 92–95; "Peter's Revelation to Take the Gospel to the Gentiles" (video), ChurchofJesusChrist.org.

ACTS 10; 11:1–18; 15

Heavenly Father teaches me line upon line through revelation.

When Peter saw the vision described in Acts 10, he struggled at first to understand it and "doubted in himself what [it] should mean" (verse 17). Yet the Lord gave Peter greater understanding as Peter sought it. As you read Acts 10, 11, and 15, notice how Peter's understanding of his vision deepened over time. How have you sought and received greater understanding from God when you had questions?

Acts 10, 11, and 15 recount instances in which the Lord directed His servants through revelation. It might help to record what you learn about revelation as you read these chapters. In what ways does the Spirit speak to you?

See also Gospel Topics, "Revelation," topics.ChurchofJesusChrist.org; Quentin L. Cook, "The Blessing of Continuing Revelation to Prophets and Personal Revelation to Guide Our Lives," *Ensign* or *Liahona*, May 2020, 96–100; "The Jerusalem Conference" (video), ChurchofJesusChrist.org.

ACTS 11:26

I am a Christian because I believe in and follow Jesus Christ.

What is significant about a person being called a Christian? (see Acts 11:26). What does it mean to you to be known as a Christian? Consider the significance of names. For instance, what does your family name mean to you? Why is the name of the Church important to you? (see Doctrine and Covenants 115:4). What does it mean to you to take upon yourself the name of Jesus Christ by covenant? (see Doctrine and Covenants 20:77).

See also Mosiah 5:7–15; Alma 46:13–15; 3 Nephi 27:3–8; Russell M. Nelson, "The Correct Name of the Church," *Ensign* or *Liahona*, Nov. 2018, 87–90.

 Ideas for Family Scripture Study and Home Evening

Acts 10:17, 20. Have we ever had spiritual experiences and later doubted what we felt or learned? What advice can we give each other that might help us overcome our doubts? (See Neil L. Andersen, "Spiritually Defining Memories," *Ensign* or *Liahona*, May 2020, 18–22.)

Acts 10:34–35. How can you teach your family that "God is no respecter of persons"? (Acts 10:34). Perhaps you could display pictures of people from different backgrounds and cultures while your family reads these verses. How should the truths in these verses influence our actions? (see, for example, "I'll Walk with You" [*Children's Songbook*, 140–41]).

Acts 12:1–17. Your family could act out the account of Peter being cast into prison and members of the Church gathering together and praying for him. When have we been blessed by prayer? Is there someone we feel inspired to pray for, such as a Church leader or loved one? What does it mean to pray "without ceasing"? (Acts 12:5; see also Alma 34:27).

Peter Delivered from Prison, by A. L. Noakes

Acts 14. As you read this chapter together, some family members could make note of blessings that came to the disciples and the Church. Other family members could note opposition or trials disciples experienced. Why does God allow difficult things to happen to righteous people?

Acts 15:1–21. These verses describe a disagreement in the Church about whether converts needed to keep the law of Moses, including circumcision. What did the Apostles do about this disagreement? What can we learn from this example about how Church leaders direct the work of the Church?

For more ideas for teaching children, see this week's outline in *Come, Follow Me—For Primary*.

Suggested song: "I'll Walk with You," *Children's Songbook*, 140–41.

Improving Our Teaching

Draw a picture. Pictures can help family members visualize scriptural teachings and stories. You could invite family members to draw pictures of what you read, such as Peter's vision in Acts 10.

The experiences of Peter and Cornelius demonstrate that "God is no respecter of persons" (Acts 10:34).

Acts 16–21

"THE LORD HAD CALLED US FOR TO PREACH THE GOSPEL"

As you read about Paul's efforts to preach the gospel, the Spirit may prompt you with thoughts or feelings. Write these promptings down, and make plans to act on them.

RECORD YOUR IMPRESSIONS

Among the Lord's final words to His Apostles was the commandment "Go ye therefore, and teach all nations, baptizing them in the name of the Father, and of the Son, and of the Holy Ghost: teaching them to observe all things whatsoever I have commanded you" (Matthew 28:19–20). While the Apostles didn't quite make it to *all* nations, Acts 16–21 does show that Paul and his companions did make remarkable progress in establishing the Church. They taught, baptized, and conferred the gift of the Holy Ghost. They performed miracles, even raising a man from the dead, and foretold the Great Apostasy (Acts 20:7–12, 28–31). And the work they started continues with living Apostles today, along with devoted disciples like you, who are helping fulfill the Savior's commission in ways Paul never could have imagined. Perhaps you are aware of people who do not know their Heavenly Father or His gospel. Perhaps you have felt that your "spirit was stirred in [you]" to share with them what you know about Him (Acts 17:16). If you follow Paul's example of humility and boldness in sharing the gospel, you may find someone "whose heart the Lord [has] opened" (Acts 16:14).

 Ideas for Personal Scripture Study

The Spirit will guide me in my efforts to share the gospel.

The Prophet Joseph Smith declared, "No man can preach the Gospel without the Holy Ghost" (*Teachings of Presidents of the Church: Joseph Smith* [2007], 332). As you read Acts 16–21, consider why the Prophet's statement is true. Note instances in which the Spirit aided Paul and his companions. What blessings came as they followed the Spirit? When have you felt the Spirit prompting you in your efforts to share the gospel?

I can declare the gospel in all circumstances.

Being thrown in prison for preaching the gospel might seem like an understandable reason to stop preaching. But to Paul and Silas, it became an opportunity to convert a jailer (see Acts 16:16–34). Throughout Acts 16–21, look for other examples of Paul's willingness to share his witness with everyone. Why do you think he was so bold and fearless? What do you learn from Paul's example?

There are many more messages about sharing the gospel in Acts 16–21. As you study these chapters, look for some that are especially applicable to you.

See also Dieter F. Uchtdorf, "Missionary Work: Sharing What Is in Your Heart," *Ensign* or *Liahona*, May 2019, 15–18.

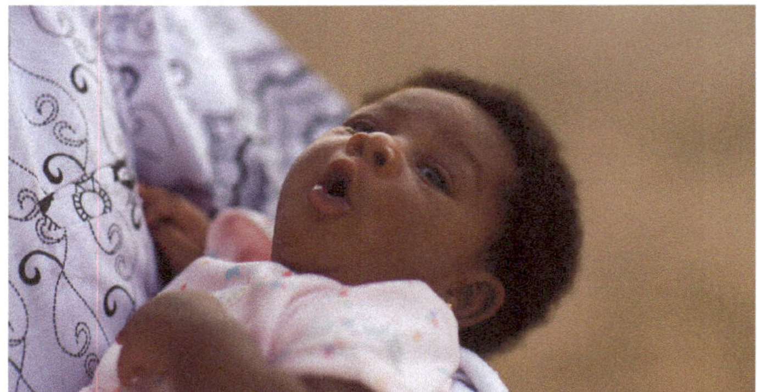

Each of us is a child of God.

"We are the offspring of God."

In Athens, Paul found people with diverse opinions and religious views. They were always seeking "to hear some new thing," and what Paul had to offer was definitely new to them (see Acts 17:19–21). They worshipped many gods, including one they called "the unknown God" (Acts 17:23), but they believed that gods were powers or forces, not living, personal beings, and certainly not our Father. Ponder what Paul said to help them come to know God. What does it mean to you to be the "offspring of God"? (Acts 17:29). In your opinion, how is being a child of God different from being just one of His creations? How does understanding this truth influence how you see yourself and others?

If you had stood beside Paul as he was testifying, what would you have told the ancient Greeks about our Heavenly Father? Do you know someone who could benefit from hearing your testimony?

See also Romans 8:16; 1 John 5:2; "We Are the Offspring of God" (video), ChurchofJesusChrist.org.

 ## Ideas for Family Scripture Study and Home Evening

Acts 16–21. To deepen your family's understanding of Acts 16–21, you could study the map at the end of this outline, looking for the cities where Paul preached the gospel in these chapters. What resources do we have today to help bring the gospel to all nations?

To inspire your family to share the gospel, you could show one or more of the videos in the "Sharing the Gospel" section of the Gospel Library.

Acts 17:10–12; 18:24–28. How can we be more like the Saints in these verses? What might it mean to "[receive] the word with all readiness of mind"? (Acts 17:11). What can we do to be "mighty in the scriptures"? (Acts 18:24).

Acts 19:1–7. These verses can help your family have a discussion about the importance of being baptized and confirmed. To better understand the truths in Acts 19:1–7, you could discuss some things that are useless without something else, such as a cell phone without a battery. Or you could share this teaching from the Prophet Joseph Smith: "Baptism by water is but half a baptism, and is good for nothing without the other half—that is, the baptism of the Holy Ghost" (*Teachings: Joseph Smith*, 95). Why is baptism "good for nothing" without receiving the gift of the Holy Ghost? (see 3 Nephi 27:19–20; Moses 6:59–61).

Acts 19:18–20. As you read Acts 19:18–20, notice the value of the possessions that the people were willing to give up in order to embrace the gospel (see verse 19). Are there worldly possessions or activities we need to give up in order to receive heavenly blessings?

Acts 20:32–35. When has your family experienced Christ's teaching that "it is more blessed to give than to receive"? (Acts 20:35). Is there someone who could benefit from service, time, or gifts that your family could give? As a family, discuss some ideas and make a plan to serve someone. How do we feel when we serve others? Why is it more blessed to give than to receive?

For more ideas for teaching children, see this week's outline in *Come, Follow Me—For Primary*.

Suggested song: "I Am a Child of God," *Children's Songbook*, 2–3.

Improving Personal Study

Record impressions. "When you record spiritual impressions, you show the Lord that you value His direction, and He will bless you with more frequent revelation" (*Teaching in the Savior's Way*, 12; see also page 30).

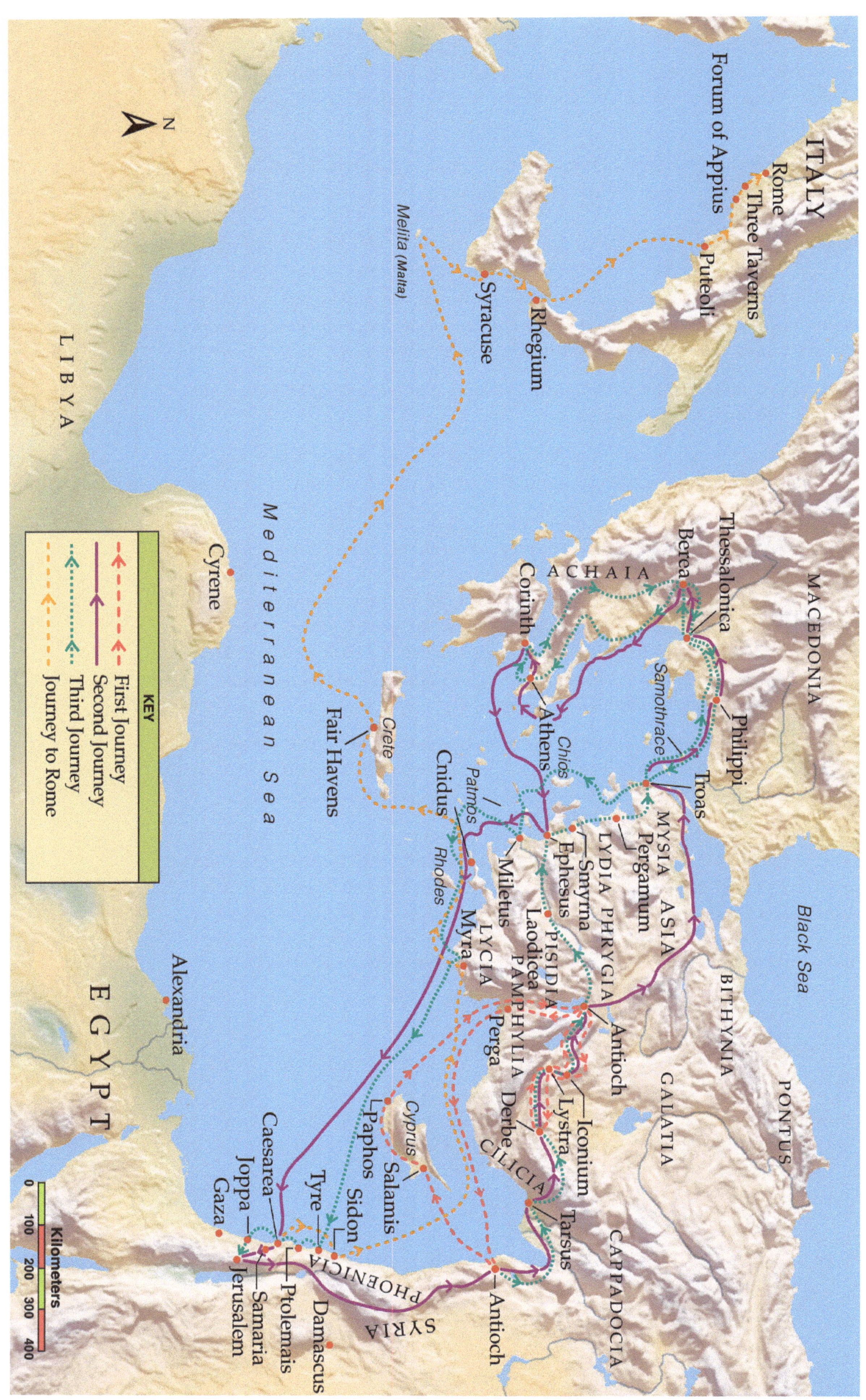

The missionary journeys of the Apostle Paul.

Acts 22–28

"A MINISTER AND A WITNESS"

Impressions from the Holy Ghost are often quiet and sometimes fleeting. Recording your impressions allows you to reflect on them more deeply. As you read Acts 22–28, write down the thoughts and feelings that come to you, and take time to ponder them.

RECORD YOUR IMPRESSIONS

"When we are on the Lord's errand," President Thomas S. Monson promised, "we are entitled to the Lord's help" ("To Learn, to Do, to Be," *Ensign* or *Liahona*, Nov. 2008, 62). We are not entitled, however, to a smooth road and an endless stream of successes. For proof of this, we need look no further than Paul the Apostle. His errand from the Savior was "to bear my name before the Gentiles, and kings, and the children of Israel" (Acts 9:15). In chapters 22–28 of Acts, we see Paul fulfilling this errand and facing great opposition—chains, imprisonment, physical abuse, a shipwreck, and even a snake attack. But we also see that Jesus "stood by him, and said, Be of good cheer, Paul" (Acts 23:11). Paul's experiences are an inspiring reminder that the Lord's call to "declare [His] gospel with the sound of rejoicing" comes with this promise: "Lift up your hearts and be glad, for I am in your midst" (Doctrine and Covenants 29:4–5; see also Matthew 28:19–20).

 Ideas for Personal Scripture Study

ACTS 22:1–21; 26:1–29

Disciples of Jesus Christ share their testimonies boldly.

When Paul delivered the powerful testimonies recorded in Acts 22 and 26, he was being held prisoner by Roman soldiers. The people he spoke to had the power to condemn him to death. Yet he chose to boldly bear witness of Jesus Christ and "the heavenly vision" (Acts 26:19) he had received. What inspires you about his words? Consider the opportunities you have to share your testimony. For example, do your friends know how you feel about Jesus Christ? Or when was the last time you told your family how you gained your testimony of the gospel?

When young Joseph Smith was ridiculed for telling about his First Vision, he was inspired by the way Paul testified of his vision (see Joseph Smith—History 1:24–25). How would you summarize what Joseph Smith learned from Paul? What do you learn from these two witnesses of Jesus Christ?

See also Neil L. Andersen, "We Talk of Christ," *Ensign* or *Liahona*, Nov. 2020, 88–91.

ACTS 23:10–11; 27:13–25, 40–44

The Lord stands by those who strive to serve Him.

As Paul's ministry clearly shows, difficulties in our lives are not a sign that God disapproves of us or the work we are doing. In fact, sometimes it is during the difficulties that we feel His support most strongly. It might be interesting to review what you've read recently about Paul's ministry and list some of the things he endured (see, for example, Acts 14:19–20; 16:19–27; 21:31–34; 23:10–11; 27:13–25, 40–44). How did the Lord stand by him? How has He stood by you?

ACTS 24:24–27; 26:1–3, 24–29; 27

There is safety and peace in heeding the words of God's servants.

Throughout his ministry, Paul bore powerful testimony of Jesus Christ and His gospel. Many people accepted his witness, but not everyone did. As you read Acts 24:24–27 and Acts 26:1–3, 24–29, look for words and phrases that show how the following Roman rulers in Judea reacted to Paul's teachings:

- Felix

- Festus

- King Agrippa

While sailing to Rome to be tried by Caesar, Paul prophesied that "hurt and much damage" would come to the ship and its passengers (Acts 27:10). Read chapter 27 to find out how Paul's shipmates reacted to his warnings. Do you find any lessons for yourself in their experience?

Have you ever reacted like any of these people when you heard the teachings of Church leaders? What are some possible consequences of reacting in these ways? What do you learn from these accounts about heeding the counsel of the Lord through His servants?

See also 2 Nephi 33:1–2; D. Todd Christofferson, "The Voice of Warning," *Ensign* or *Liahona*, May 2017, 108–11; "Follow the Living Prophet," *Teachings of Presidents of the Church: Ezra Taft Benson* (2014), 147–55.

Ideas for Family Scripture Study and Home Evening

Acts 24:16. Before his conversion, Paul had a long history of offenses toward God. But because he was willing to repent, he was able to say, "Herein do I exercise myself, to have always a conscience void of offence toward God, and toward men" (see also Doctrine and Covenants 135:4–5). How can we rid our conscience of offenses toward God and others?

Acts 26:16–18. In these verses, what did the Lord call Paul to do? What opportunities do we have to do similar things?

Acts 28:1–9. Does anyone in your family like snakes? You may want to ask that person or another family member to tell the stories found in Acts 28:1–9. Your children might enjoy drawing a picture of these stories or acting them out. What lessons can we learn from these accounts? One might be that the Lord fulfills His promises to His servants. For example, you could compare the promises made in Mark 16:18 with their fulfillments in Paul's experiences. You could also find in a recent general conference address a promise made by one of the Lord's servants—perhaps one that is meaningful to your family—and display it in your home. How can we show our faith that this promise will be fulfilled?

God protected Paul when a venomous snake bit him.

Acts 28:22–24. Like the Church in Paul's day (called a "sect" in verse 22), the Church today is often "spoken against." When people spoke against the Savior and His Church, how did Paul respond? What can we learn from Paul's experience?

For more ideas for teaching children, see this week's outline in *Come, Follow Me—For Primary*.

Suggested hymn: "My Redeemer Lives," *Hymns*, no. 135.

Improving Our Teaching

Focus on principles that will bless your family. As you study the scriptures, ask yourself, "What do I find here that will be especially meaningful to my family?" (See *Teaching in the Savior's Way*, 17.)

Paul before King Agrippa. *Valiant in the Testimony of Jesus Christ,* by Daniel A. Lewis

Romans 1–6

"THE POWER OF GOD UNTO SALVATION"

Recording promptings will help you remember what the Spirit is teaching you. Consider also recording how you feel about these promptings.

RECORD YOUR IMPRESSIONS

By the time Paul wrote his epistle to Roman Church members, who were a diverse group of Jews and Gentiles, the Church of Jesus Christ had grown far beyond a small band of believers from Galilee. About 20 years after the Savior's Resurrection, there were congregations of Christians almost everywhere the Apostles could reasonably travel—including Rome, the capital of a powerful empire. Still, compared to the vastness of the Roman empire, the Church was small and often the object of persecution. In such conditions, some might feel "ashamed of the gospel of Christ"—but, of course, not Paul. He knew and testified that true power, "the power of God unto salvation," is found in the gospel of Jesus Christ (Romans 1:16).

 Ideas for Personal Scripture Study

What are the Epistles, and how are they organized?

The Epistles are letters written by Church leaders to Saints in various parts of the world. The Apostle Paul wrote most of the epistles in the New Testament—starting with Romans and ending with Hebrews. His epistles are organized by length, except for Hebrews (see Bible Dictionary, "Pauline Epistles"). Although Romans is the first epistle in the New Testament, it was actually written near the end of Paul's missionary journeys.

ROMANS 1–6

"The just shall live by faith."

The following definitions may help you better understand the Epistle to the Romans:

The law. When Paul wrote of "the law," he was referring to the law of Moses. The word "works" in Paul's writings referred to outward actions associated with the law of Moses. Consider how the law of Moses and the works required under it are different from "the law of faith" described in Romans 3:23–31.

Circumcision, uncircumcision. Anciently, circumcision was a token or symbol of the covenant God made with Abraham. Paul used the term "circumcision" to refer to Jews (the covenant people) and "uncircumcision" to refer to Gentiles. Ponder what Romans 2:25–29 teaches about what it really means to be God's covenant people. Note that circumcision is no longer a token of God's covenant with His people (see Acts 15:23–29).

Justification, justify, justified. These terms refer to the remission, or pardoning, of sin. When we are justified, we are forgiven, declared guiltless, and freed from eternal punishment for our sins. When you see these terms, notice what Paul taught about what makes justification possible (see also Guide to the Scriptures, "Justification, Justify," scriptures.ChurchofJesusChrist.org; D. Todd Christofferson, "Justification and Sanctification," *Ensign*, June 2001, 18–25). In Romans, words like "righteous" and "righteousness" can be seen as synonyms for words like "just" and "justification."

Grace. Grace is "divine . . . help or strength, given through the bounteous mercy and love of Jesus Christ." Through grace, all people will be resurrected and receive immortality. In addition, "grace is an enabling power that allows men and women to lay hold on eternal life and exaltation after they have expended their own best efforts." We do not earn grace through our efforts; rather, it is grace that gives us "strength and assistance to do good works that [we] otherwise would not be able to maintain" (Bible Dictionary, "Grace"; see also 2 Nephi 25:23; Dieter F. Uchtdorf, "The Gift of Grace," *Ensign* or *Liahona*, May 2015, 107–10; Brad Wilcox, "His Grace Is Sufficient," *Ensign*, Sept. 2013, 35–37; or *Liahona*, Sept. 2013, 43–45). As you read Romans, record what you learn about the Savior's grace.

ROMANS 2:17–29

My actions should reflect and increase my conversion.

Some of the Jewish Christians in Rome apparently still believed that the rites and rituals of the law of Moses brought salvation. This may seem like a problem that doesn't apply anymore since we don't live by the law of Moses. But as you read Paul's writings, especially Romans 2:17–29, think about your own efforts to live the gospel. Are your outward performances, such as taking the sacrament or attending the temple, deepening your conversion and strengthening your faith in Christ? (see Alma 25:15–16). Is there something you should change so that your outward actions are leading to a change of heart?

See also Dallin H. Oaks, "The Challenge to Become," *Ensign*, Nov. 2000, 32–34.

ROMANS 3:10–31; 5

Through Jesus Christ, I can be forgiven of my sins.

Some people may feel discouraged at Paul's bold declaration that "there is none righteous, no, not one" (Romans 3:10). But there are also hopeful messages in Romans. Look for them in chapters 3 and 5, and consider why remembering that "all have sinned, and come short of the glory of God" (Romans 3:23) is an important step toward learning to "rejoice in hope" through Jesus Christ (Romans 5:2).

ROMANS 6

Jesus Christ invites me to "walk in newness of life."

Paul taught that the gospel of Jesus Christ should change the way we live. What statements in Romans 6 describe how following the Savior has helped you "walk in newness of life"? (verse 4).

 ## Ideas for Family Scripture Study and Home Evening

Romans 1:16–17. How can we show that we are "not ashamed of the gospel of Christ"?

Romans 3:23–28. As you read these verses, you might discuss the difference between "earning" God's grace, which we can never do, and receiving it, which we must do. When have we felt God's grace? How can we receive it more completely?

Romans 5:3–5. What tribulations have we experienced? How have these tribulations helped us to develop patience, experience, and hope?

Romans 6:3–6. What did Paul say in these verses about the symbolism of baptism? Perhaps your family could plan to attend an upcoming baptism. Or someone in your family could share pictures or memories from his or her baptism. How does making and keeping our baptismal covenants help us "walk in newness of life"?

Baptism symbolizes beginning a new life as a disciple of Christ.

For more ideas for teaching children, see this week's outline in *Come, Follow Me—For Primary*.

Suggested song: "When I Am Baptized," *Children's Songbook*, 103.

Improving Personal Study

Ask questions as you study. As you study the scriptures, questions may come to mind. Ponder these questions and look for answers. For example, in Romans 1–6 you could look for answers to the question "What is grace?"

Be Not Afraid, by Greg K. Olsen

Romans 7–16

"OVERCOME EVIL WITH GOOD"

Only a few of the gospel principles in Romans 7–16 can be included in this outline, so don't limit yourself to what is addressed here. Pay attention to the inspiration you receive as you study.

RECORD YOUR IMPRESSIONS

As he opened his epistle to the Romans, Paul greeted Church members by calling them "beloved of God" who were "called to be saints." He remarked that their "faith [was] spoken of throughout the whole world" (Romans 1:7–8). Even though Paul spent much of his epistle correcting false ideas and flawed behaviors, it seems he also wanted to assure these new Christian converts that they truly were Saints who were beloved of God. His tender counsel blesses all of us who struggle to feel God's love and for whom becoming a Saint may feel out of reach. With humble empathy, Paul acknowledged that he had felt like a "wretched man" at times (Romans 7:24), but the gospel of Jesus Christ had given him power to overcome sin (see Joseph Smith Translation, Romans 7:22–27 [in the Bible appendix]). With that power, the Savior's redeeming power, we can "overcome evil"—both evil in the world and evil in ourselves—"with good" (Romans 12:21).

 Ideas for Personal Scripture Study

ROMANS 7–8

Those who follow the Spirit can become "joint-heirs with Christ."

Even after entering into "newness of life" through the ordinance of baptism (Romans 6:4), perhaps you have felt some of the inner conflict Paul described in Romans 7—the "warring" between the natural man and your righteous desires (Romans 7:23). But Paul also spoke of hope in Romans 8:23–25. What reasons for this hope do you find in chapter 8? You might also look for blessings that come from having "the Spirit of God dwell in you" (Romans 8:9). How can you seek the companionship of the Holy Ghost more fully in your life?

ROMANS 8:16–39

The gift of eternal glory far outweighs my trials on earth.

Just a few years after Paul wrote this epistle, the Saints in Rome suffered horrific persecutions. What do you find in Romans 8:16–39 that might have helped these Saints when persecution came? How might these words apply to you and the trials you currently face?

Look for connections between these verses and this counsel from Sister Linda S. Reeves: "I do not know why we have the many trials that we have, but it is my personal feeling that the reward is so great, so eternal and everlasting, so joyful and beyond our understanding that in that day of reward, we may feel to say to our merciful, loving Father, 'Was that *all* that was required?' I believe that if we could daily remember and recognize the depth of that love our Heavenly Father and our Savior have for us, we would be willing to do anything to be back in Their presence again, surrounded by Their love eternally. What will it matter . . . what we suffered here if, in the end, those trials are the very things which qualify us for eternal life and exaltation in the kingdom of God with our Father and Savior?" ("Worthy of Our Promised Blessings," *Ensign* or *Liahona*, Nov. 2015, 11). Decide what you will do to "daily remember and recognize" God's love for you.

ROMANS 8:29–30; 9–11

What did Paul mean by "predestinate," "election," and "foreknow"?

Paul used the terms "predestinate," "election," and "foreknow" to teach that before this life, God chose some of His children to be part of Israel, His covenant people. This meant they would receive special blessings and responsibilities so they could bless all the people of the world (see Guide to the Scriptures, "Election," scriptures.ChurchofJesusChrist.org). However, Paul emphasized in Romans 9–11 that *all* of God's children can become His covenant people, and we all receive eternal life the same way—through faith in Jesus Christ and obedience to His commandments.

See also Ephesians 1:3–4; 1 Peter 1:2; Alma 13:1–5; Gospel Topics, "Foreordination," topics.ChurchofJesusChrist.org.

ROMANS 12–16

Paul invites me to become a true Saint and follower of Jesus Christ.

The last five chapters of Romans contain dozens of specific instructions about living as Saints. One way to study these instructions is to look for topics that are repeated. How would you summarize Paul's counsel?

You may not be able to apply all of this counsel at once, but the Spirit can help you find one or two principles you could start working on today. Share your desires with your Heavenly Father in prayer, and ask for His help.

 ## Ideas for Family Scripture Study and Home Evening

Romans 8:31–39. What do we find in Romans 8:31–39 that teaches how Heavenly Father and Jesus feel about us? When have we felt God's love?

To illustrate verses 38–39, family members could find examples of things that, like us and God's love, cannot be separated.

Elder Wilford W. Andersen taught, "The music of the gospel is [a] joyful spiritual feeling."

Romans 9:31–32. Elder Wilford W. Andersen's message "The Music of the Gospel" (*Ensign* or *Liahona*, May 2015, 54–56; see also the video on ChurchofJesusChrist.org) can help illustrate what Paul teaches about the law, works, and faith. After discussing his talk, your family could try to dance with and without music. How can faith help us experience the joy of the gospel?

Romans 10:17. Label several glasses of water with sources of the word of God (like the scriptures, personal revelation, and general conference). Discuss how the word of God increases our faith as you pour each glass into a container labeled "Faith."

Romans 12. What does it mean to make ourselves "a living sacrifice, holy, acceptable unto God"? (verse 1).

Romans 14:13–21. Your family might benefit from studying Paul's counsel about judging and arguing over personal preferences. Perhaps you could discuss appropriate ways to respond when other people, including family members, make choices that differ from yours. How can we "follow after the things which make for peace"? (verse 19).

For more ideas for teaching children, see this week's outline in *Come, Follow Me—For Primary*.

Suggested song: "I Feel My Savior's Love," *Children's Songbook*, 74–75.

Improving Our Teaching

Let children express their creativity. "When you invite children to create something related to a gospel principle, you help them better understand the principle. . . . Allow them to build, draw, color, write, and create" (*Teaching in the Savior's Way*, 25).

Abide with Me, by Del Parson

1 Corinthians 1–7

"BE PERFECTLY JOINED TOGETHER"

Record your impressions while you read 1 Corinthians 1–7. These impressions may include promptings to study an idea further, to share with others something you learn, or to make changes in your life.

RECORD YOUR IMPRESSIONS

During the months that Paul spent in Corinth, "many of the Corinthians hearing [him] believed, and were baptized" (Acts 18:8). So it must have been heartbreaking for Paul to hear, just a few years later, that there were "divisions" and "contentions" among the Corinthian Saints and that in his absence they began to heed the "wisdom of this world" (1 Corinthians 1:10–11, 20). In response, Paul wrote the letter we now call 1 Corinthians. It is full of profound doctrine, and yet at the same time, Paul seemed disappointed that the Saints were not ready to receive all the doctrine he wanted to give them. "I, brethren, could not speak unto you as unto spiritual," he lamented, "for ye are yet carnal" (1 Corinthians 3:1–3). As we prepare to read Paul's words, it might be helpful to examine our own readiness to receive truth—including our willingness to heed the Spirit and strive for unity within our families, with our fellow Saints, and with God.

Ideas for Personal Scripture Study

The members of Christ's Church strive to be united.

We don't know all the details about the lack of unity among the Corinthian Saints, but we do know about lack of unity in our *own* relationships. Think of a relationship in your life that could benefit from more unity; then look for what Paul taught in 1 Corinthians 1:10–17; 3:1–11 about lack of unity among the Corinthian Saints. What insights can you gain about how to develop greater unity with others?

See also Mosiah 18:21; 4 Nephi 1:15–17; Doctrine and Covenants 38:23–27; 105:1–5; Gospel Topics, "Unity," topics.ChurchofJesusChrist.org.

1 CORINTHIANS 1:17–31; 2

To accomplish God's work, I need the wisdom of God.

While it's good—even encouraged—to seek wisdom wherever we can find it (see 2 Nephi 9:29; Doctrine and Covenants 88:118), Paul gave some strongly worded warnings about flawed human wisdom, which he called "the wisdom of this world." As you read 1 Corinthians 1:17–25, ponder what this phrase might mean. What do you think Paul meant by the "wisdom of God"? Why do we need God's wisdom to accomplish God's work?

In your efforts to fulfill your responsibilities in accomplishing God's work, have you ever experienced the "fear, and . . . much trembling" that Paul felt when he taught the Corinthian Saints? (1 Corinthians 2:3). What do you find in 1 Corinthians 2:1–5 that gives you courage? Consider how you can show that you trust the "power of God" more than "the wisdom of men."

See also Doctrine and Covenants 1:17–28.

1 CORINTHIANS 2:9–16

I need the Holy Ghost in order to understand the things of God.

If you wanted to learn more about something like automotive mechanics or medieval architecture, how would you do it? According to 1 Corinthians 2:9–16, how is learning "the things of God" different from learning the "things of a man"? Why must we have the Holy Ghost in order to understand the things of God? After reading these verses, what do you feel you should do to understand spiritual things more fully? How could Paul's words help someone who is struggling with his or her testimony?

1 CORINTHIANS 6:13–20

My body is sacred.

Most people in Corinth felt that sexual immorality was acceptable and that their bodies were made primarily for pleasure. In other words, Corinth was not that different from the world today. What did Paul teach in 1 Corinthians 6:13–20 that could help you explain to others why you want to live a chaste life?

Like Paul, Sister Wendy W. Nelson encouraged Saints to be chaste; see her message "Love and Marriage" (worldwide devotional for young adults, Jan. 8, 2017, broadcasts.ChurchofJesusChrist .org). According to Sister Nelson, what blessings come from living the Lord's standards concerning love and intimacy?

1 CORINTHIANS 7:29–33

Did Paul teach that it is better to be unmarried than married?

Several verses in 1 Corinthians 7 seem to suggest that while marriage is acceptable, remaining single and abstaining completely from sexual relations is preferred. However, Joseph Smith Translation, 1 Corinthians 7:29–33 (in the Bible appendix) helps us understand that Paul was referring to those called to be full-time missionaries, observing that they were able to serve

God better if they remained single during their missions. The Lord has taught through His servants, including Paul, that marriage is part of His eternal plan and necessary for exaltation (see 1 Corinthians 11:11; Doctrine and Covenants 131:1–4).

 ## Ideas for Family Scripture Study and Home Evening

1 Corinthians 1:10–17; 3:1–11. As your family members read these verses, invite them to find an insight that can help them be more unified.

1 Corinthians 3:1–2. Maybe you could read these verses while eating milk and meat. You could compare the way babies grow into adults with the way we grow spiritually.

1 Corinthians 3:4–9. Paul compared his missionary efforts to planting seeds. What does his comparison teach us about sharing the gospel?

1 Corinthians 6:19–20. Comparing our bodies to temples, as Paul did, can be an effective way to teach about the sacredness of our bodies. Perhaps you could show pictures of temples, such as those that accompany this outline. Why are temples sacred? How are our bodies like temples? What can we do to treat our bodies like temples? (See also the August 2020 special edition of the *Ensign* or *Liahona* about sexuality.)

For more ideas for teaching children, see this week's outline in *Come, Follow Me—For Primary*.

Suggested song: "The Lord Gave Me a Temple," *Children's Songbook*, 153.

Improving Personal Study

Be patient with yourself. Paul taught that milk comes before meat when we are learning the gospel (see 1 Corinthians 3:1–2). If you find that some doctrines are difficult to understand now, be patient. Trust that answers will come as you have faith and diligently study.

Paul compared our bodies to the sacredness of the temple. Clockwise from upper left: Curitiba Brazil Temple, Mexico City Mexico Temple, Tokyo Japan Temple, Accra Ghana Temple.

1 Corinthians 8–13

"YE ARE THE BODY OF CHRIST"

As you prayerfully read 1 Corinthians 8–13, the Holy Ghost may speak to you in subtle ways (see 1 Kings 19:11–12). Recording these impressions will help you recall the feelings and thoughts you had during your study.

RECORD YOUR IMPRESSIONS

In Paul's time, Corinth was a wealthy trade center with residents from all over the Roman Empire. With so many different cultures and religions in the city, Church members in Corinth struggled to maintain unity, so Paul sought to help them find unity in their belief in Christ. This unity was to be more than just peaceful coexistence; Paul wasn't asking them merely to tolerate each other's differences. Rather, he taught that when you join the Church of Jesus Christ, you are "baptized into one body," and every body part is needed (1 Corinthians 12:13). When one member is lost, it's like losing a limb, and the body is weaker as a result. When one member suffers, we should all feel it and do our part to relieve it. In this kind of unity, differences are not just acknowledged but cherished, because without members of diverse gifts and abilities, the body would be limited. So whether you feel like you've always been at home in the Church or find yourself wondering if you truly belong, Paul's message to you is that unity is not sameness. You need your fellow Saints, and your fellow Saints need you.

 Ideas for Personal Scripture Study

1 CORINTHIANS 10:1–13

God provides a way to escape temptation.

Spiritual experiences, even miraculous ones, do not exempt us from temptations that are "common to man" (1 Corinthians 10:13). That may be one reason Paul wrote about how the Israelites in Moses's day struggled with temptation, even though they witnessed mighty miracles (see Exodus 13:21; 14:13–31). As you read 1 Corinthians 10:1–13, what warnings in the Israelites' experiences seem applicable to you? What kinds of "escape" from temptation has Heavenly Father provided for you? (see also Alma 13:27–30; 3 Nephi 18:18–19).

1 CORINTHIANS 10:16–17; 11:16–30

The sacrament unifies us as members of Christ's Church.

Although the sacrament involves a personal commitment between you and the Lord, it is also an experience you share with others. We almost always partake of the sacrament together, as a body of Saints. Read what Paul taught about the sacrament, and think about how this sacred ordinance can help "many" become "one" in Christ (1 Corinthians 10:17). How does partaking of the sacrament help you feel closer to Christ and other believers? How do these verses influence your feelings about the sacrament and the way you prepare for it?

1 CORINTHIANS 11:11

In God's plan, men and women need each other.

In 1 Corinthians 11:4–15, Paul referred to cultural customs that we do not follow today. However, Paul also taught an important truth that applies eternally, found in verse 11. What do you think this verse means, and why is it important? Elder David A. Bednar taught, "The man and the woman are intended to learn from, strengthen, bless, and complete each other" ("We Believe in Being Chaste," *Ensign* or *Liahona*, May 2013, 42). How should this truth influence a marriage? How should it affect the way we serve in the Church?

See also Jean B. Bingham, "United in Accomplishing God's Work," *Ensign* or *Liahona*, May 2020, 60–63.

1 CORINTHIANS 12–13

Spiritual gifts are given to benefit all of Heavenly Father's children.

The list of spiritual gifts in 1 Corinthians 12–13 is not exhaustive. But it is a good place to start as you identify and ponder the spiritual gifts Heavenly Father has given you. The article "Spiritual Gifts" in Gospel Topics (topics.ChurchofJesusChrist.org) may help you understand these gifts better. As you read Paul's list of gifts, you might add some you have noticed in others, in yourself, or in people in the scriptures. If you have a patriarchal blessing, it may mention some of your spiritual gifts. How do these gifts help you bless others? Consider how you can seek "earnestly the best gifts" (1 Corinthians 12:31).

See also 1 Corinthians 14; Moroni 10:8–21, 30; Doctrine and Covenants 46:8–26; Articles of Faith 1:7.

Ideas for Family Scripture Study and Home Evening

1 Corinthians 9:24–27. Since Paul compared living the gospel to running a race, you could have a family race to illustrate his point. Award a crown to everyone who finishes the race, and discuss how all who are diligent in following Jesus Christ in this life will win the "incorruptible" prize (1 Corinthians 9:25; see also 2 Timothy 4:7–8). What does a runner do to prepare for a race? What can we do to prepare to return to Heavenly Father?

Paul compared living the gospel to running a race.

1 Corinthians 12:1–11. After reading these verses together, consider giving everyone a piece of paper with the name of another family member at the top. Ask everyone to list the spiritual gifts they notice that person has. You could then pass the papers in a circle until everyone has had a chance to write about each family member's gifts.

1 Corinthians 12:3. Why is the Holy Ghost necessary to gain a testimony of Jesus Christ? What can we do to invite the Holy Ghost to strengthen our testimonies of Him?

1 Corinthians 12:12–27. Paul's analogy of a body could be a memorable way to discuss family unity. For example, family members could try drawing a body made only of eyes or ears (see verse 17). What do these verses suggest about how we should treat each other as family members?

1 Corinthians 13:4–8. Paul's definition of charity might make an inspiring motto for your family. You could assign each family member to study a phrase in verses 4–8 and teach the rest of the family what it means using definitions, examples, and personal experiences. How is the Savior an example of these attributes? You could also make posters together for each of these phrases and display them throughout your house. Be creative!

For more ideas for teaching children, see this week's outline in *Come, Follow Me—For Primary*.

Suggested song: "Love Is Spoken Here," *Children's Songbook*, 190–91.

Improving Our Teaching

Display a scripture. Display a verse you find meaningful in a place where family members will see it often. Invite other family members to take turns selecting a scripture to display.

"The bread which we break, is it not the communion of the body of Christ? For we being many are one bread, and one body" (1 Corinthians 10:16–17).

1 Corinthians 14–16

"GOD IS NOT THE AUTHOR OF CONFUSION, BUT OF PEACE"

Record your impressions while you read 1 Corinthians 14–16. Pray about what the Spirit has taught you, and ask Heavenly Father if there is more He would like you to learn.

RECORD YOUR IMPRESSIONS

Because the Church and its doctrines were relatively new in Corinth, it's understandable that Corinthian Saints encountered confusion. Paul had previously taught them the fundamental truth of the gospel: "That Christ died for our sins . . . and that he was buried, and that he rose again the third day" (1 Corinthians 15:3–4). But some members soon began teaching that "there is no resurrection of the dead" (1 Corinthians 15:12). Paul implored them to "keep in memory" the truths they had been taught (1 Corinthians 15:2). When we encounter conflicting opinions about gospel truths, it is good to remember that "God is not the author of confusion, but of peace" (1 Corinthians 14:33). Listening to the Lord's appointed servants and holding to the simple truths they repeatedly teach can help us find peace and "stand fast in the faith" (1 Corinthians 16:13).

 Ideas for Personal Scripture Study

1 CORINTHIANS 14

I can seek the gift of prophecy.

What is the gift of prophecy? Is it the ability to predict the future? Is it just for prophets? Or can anyone receive this gift?

Ponder these questions as you study 1 Corinthians 14:3, 31, 39–40. You could also read Revelation 19:10 and "Prophecy, Prophesy" in Guide to the Scriptures (scriptures.ChurchofJesusChrist .org). Based on what you learn, how would you define the gift of prophecy? What might Paul have meant when he invited the Corinthians to "covet to prophesy"? (1 Corinthians 14:39). How can you accept this invitation?

See also Joel 2:28–29; Alma 17:3; Doctrine and Covenants 11:23–28.

1 CORINTHIANS 14:34–35

How does the statement about women in these verses apply today?

In Paul's day, there were different expectations about how women participated in society, including in church meetings. Whatever the teachings in 1 Corinthians 14:34–35 meant in Paul's day, they shouldn't be understood to mean that women cannot speak and lead in the Church today (see Joseph Smith Translation, 1 Corinthians 14:34 [in 1 Corinthians 14:34, footnote *b*]). President Russell M. Nelson said to the women of the Church today: "We . . . need your strength, your conversion, your conviction, your ability to lead, your wisdom, and your voices. The kingdom of God is not and cannot be complete without women who make sacred covenants and then keep them, women who can speak with the power and authority of God!" ("A Plea to My Sisters," *Ensign* or *Liahona*, Nov. 2015, 96).

1 CORINTHIANS 15:1–34, 53–58

Jesus Christ gained victory over death.

The Resurrection of Jesus Christ is so fundamental to Christianity, one might say that without it there *is* no Christianity—to use Paul's words, "then is our preaching vain, and your faith is also vain" (1 Corinthians 15:14). Yet some of the Corinthian Saints were teaching that there would be "no resurrection of the dead" (1 Corinthians 15:12). As you read Paul's response in 1 Corinthians 15, take a moment to ponder how your life would be different if you did not believe in the Resurrection (see 2 Nephi 9:6–19; Alma 40:19–23; Doctrine and Covenants 93:33–34). What does the phrase "If Christ be not raised, your faith is vain" mean to you? (verse 17).

It is also worth noting that Paul referred to baptism for the dead as evidence for the reality of the resurrection (see 1 Corinthians 15:29). How has temple and family history work strengthened your faith in the doctrine of resurrection?

See also Doctrine and Covenants 138:11–37.

1 CORINTHIANS 15:35–54

Resurrected bodies are different from mortal bodies.

Have you ever wondered what a resurrected body is like? According to 1 Corinthians 15:35, some of the Corinthians wondered the same thing. Read Paul's answer in verses 36–54, and note words and phrases that describe the differences between mortal bodies and resurrected bodies. As you do, you might compare verses 40–42 with Doctrine and Covenants 76:50–112. What does this revelation to the Prophet Joseph Smith add to your understanding? (see also Joseph Smith Translation, 1 Corinthians 15:40 [in 1 Corinthians 15:40, footnote *a*]). Why are these truths valuable to you?

See also Luke 24:39; Alma 11:43–45; Doctrine and Covenants 88:14–33.

"There is one glory of the sun" (1 Corinthians 15:41).

Ideas for Family Scripture Study and Home Evening

1 Corinthians 15:29. We learn from verse 29 that ancient Christians participated in baptisms for the dead, just as we do today. How would we explain to others why we are baptized for our ancestors? (see "What Are Baptisms for the Dead?" [video], ChurchofJesusChrist.org). What are we doing as a family to provide temple ordinances for our deceased ancestors who need them? You can find more resources on this topic in the Gospel Topics article "Baptisms for the Dead" (topics.ChurchofJesusChrist.org) and at FamilySearch.org.

1 Corinthians 15:35–54. What objects or pictures could you show to help your family understand some of the terms Paul used to describe how mortal bodies are different from resurrected bodies? For instance, to demonstrate the difference between *corruptible* and *incorruptible* (see verses 52–54) you could show metal that has rusted and metal that doesn't rust. Or you could contrast something weak with something powerful (see verse 43).

1 Corinthians 15:55–57. A discussion about these verses can be especially meaningful if your family knows someone who has passed away. Family members could bear testimony of how Jesus Christ takes away "the sting of death" (verse 56).

1 Corinthians 16:13. To help your family members relate to this verse, you could draw a circle on the ground and instruct a family member to "stand fast" inside it with his or her eyes closed. Then others could try to push or pull him or her from the circle. What difference does it make when the person in the circle has his or her eyes open and can "watch"? What can we do to "stand strong" when we are tempted to make bad choices? (see also "Stay in the Boat and Hold On!" [video], ChurchofJesusChrist.org).

For more ideas for teaching children, see this week's outline in *Come, Follow Me—For Primary*.

Suggested hymn: "He Is Risen!," *Hymns*, no. 199.

Improving Personal Study

Look for patterns. In the scriptures we find patterns that show how the Lord does His work. What patterns do you find in 1 Corinthians 14 that help us understand how to edify one another?

Why Weepest Thou?, © Simon Dewey 2021. Used with permission from Altus Fine Art/www.altusfineart.com

2 Corinthians 1–7

"BE YE RECONCILED TO GOD"

As you study Paul's letters to the Corinthians, write down some of the gospel principles you discover and ponder how you can apply them in your life.

RECORD YOUR IMPRESSIONS

Sometimes, being a Church leader means having to say some difficult things. This was true in Paul's day just as it is today. Apparently a previous letter from Paul to the Corinthian Saints included chastening and caused hurt feelings. In the letter that became 2 Corinthians, he tried to explain what had motivated his harsh words: "Out of much affliction and anguish of heart I wrote to you with many tears; not that ye should be grieved, but that ye might know the love which I have more abundantly unto you" (2 Corinthians 2:4). When you're on the receiving end of some correction from a leader, it definitely helps to know that it is inspired by Christlike love. And even in those cases where it is not, if we're willing to see others with the kind of love Paul felt, it's easier to respond appropriately to any offenses. As Elder Jeffrey R. Holland counseled, "Be kind regarding human frailty—your own as well as that of those who serve with you in a Church led by volunteer, mortal men and women. Except in the case of His only perfect Begotten Son, imperfect people are all God has ever had to work with" ("Lord, I Believe," *Ensign* or *Liahona*, May 2013, 94).

 Ideas for Personal Scripture Study

2 CORINTHIANS 1:3–7; 4:6–10, 17–18; 7:4–7

My trials can be a blessing.

Given everything Paul faced during his life, it's not surprising that he wrote a lot about the purposes and blessings of tribulation. As you read 2 Corinthians 1:3–7; 4:6–10, 17–18; 7:4–7, think about ways your trials can be a blessing. For example, you might ponder how God "comforteth [you] in all [your] tribulation" and how you can, in turn, "comfort them which are in any trouble" (2 Corinthians 1:4). Or you might focus on how the light of Jesus Christ "hath shined" in your heart, even when you were "troubled" and "perplexed" (2 Corinthians 4:6, 8).

See also Mosiah 24:13–17; Henry B. Eyring, "Tested, Proved, and Polished," *Ensign* or *Liahona*, Nov. 2020, 96–99; Gospel Topics, "Adversity," topics.ChurchofJesusChrist.org.

2 CORINTHIANS 2:5–11

Forgiveness is a blessing I can both give and receive.

We don't know much about the man Paul referred to in 2 Corinthians 2:5–11—only that he had transgressed (see verses 5–6) and that Paul wanted the Saints to forgive him (see verses 7–8). Why do we sometimes fail to "confirm [our] love toward" a loved one who has offended us? (verse 8). How does withholding forgiveness harm others and ourselves? (see verses 7, 10–11). How does withholding forgiveness give "Satan . . . an advantage of us"? (verse 11).

See also Doctrine and Covenants 64:9–11.

2 CORINTHIANS 5:14–21

Through the Atonement of Jesus Christ, I can be reconciled to God.

As much as anyone, Paul knew what it was like to become "a new creature" (2 Corinthians 5:17). He went from being a persecutor of the Christians to a fearless defender of Christ. As you read 2 Corinthians 5:14–21, think about questions like these: What does it mean to reconcile? What does it mean to be reconciled to God? Ponder what might be separating you from God. What do you need to do to be more completely reconciled with Him? How does the Savior make that possible?

You might also ponder what it means to be "ambassadors for Christ" in "the ministry of reconciliation" (verses 18, 20). What insights do you gain from Elder Jeffrey R. Holland's message "The Ministry of Reconciliation"? (*Ensign* or *Liahona*, Nov. 2018, 77–79).

See also 2 Nephi 10:23–25.

2 CORINTHIANS 7:8–11

Godly sorrow leads to repentance.

We don't usually think of sorrow as a good thing, but Paul spoke of "godly sorrow" (2 Corinthians 7:10) as an important part of repentance. Consider what you learn about godly sorrow from the following: 2 Corinthians 7:8–11; Alma 36:16–21; Mormon 2:11–15; and Sister Michelle D. Craig's message "Divine Discontent" (*Ensign* or *Liahona*, Nov. 2018, 52–55). When have you felt godly sorrow, and what effect did it have in your life?

 Ideas for Family Scripture Study and Home Evening

2 Corinthians 3:1–3. Have members of your family ever asked someone to write a letter of recommendation for them, such as for a job or school application? Ask them to talk about this experience. Paul taught that the lives of the Saints were like letters of recommendation for the gospel of Jesus Christ, "written not with ink, but with the Spirit of the living God." As you read 2 Corinthians 3:1–3 together, discuss how our examples are like letters that can be "known and read of all men," demonstrating the truth and worth of the gospel. Perhaps each family member could write a letter or "epistle" explaining how another family member has been a good example of a disciple of Jesus Christ. They could read their letters to the family and give them to the family member they wrote about. Why is it important to understand that our lives are "epistle[s] of Christ"?

2 Corinthians 5:6–7. What does it mean to "walk by faith, not by sight"? What are we doing to show that we believe in the Savior even though we can't see Him?

2 Corinthians 5:17. Can your family think of or find examples in nature of things that go through remarkable transformations and become new creatures? (see the picture at the end of this outline). How can the gospel of Jesus Christ change us?

2 Corinthians 6:1–10. According to 2 Corinthians 6:1–10, what does it mean to be "ministers of God"? (verse 4). What qualities does a minister of God have?

2 Corinthians 6:14–18. How can we follow Paul's counsel to "come out from among [the unrighteous], and be ye separate," while also loving those around us?

For more ideas for teaching children, see this week's outline in *Come, Follow Me—For Primary*.

Suggested song: "Help Me, Dear Father," *Children's Songbook*, 99.

Improving Our Teaching

Share object lessons. Some gospel concepts, such as the Atonement, can be difficult to understand. Consider using pictures or objects that can help your family understand the principles you discover in the scriptures.

When we are converted to the gospel of Christ, our transformation is so profound that Paul described it as becoming a "new creature" (2 Corinthians 5:17).

2 Corinthians 8–13

"GOD LOVETH A CHEERFUL GIVER"

Recording spiritual impressions will help you remember what you learn during scripture study. You might write in a study journal, make notes in the margins of your scriptures, add notes in your Gospel Library app, or make an audio recording of your thoughts.

RECORD YOUR IMPRESSIONS ____

What would you do if you heard that a congregation of Saints in another area was struggling in poverty? This was the situation that Paul described to the Corinthian Saints in 2 Corinthians 8–9. He hoped to persuade the Corinthian Saints to donate some of their abundance to Saints in need. But beyond a request for donations, Paul's words also contain profound truths about giving: "Every man according as he purposeth in his heart, so let him give; not grudgingly, or of necessity: for God loveth a cheerful giver" (2 Corinthians 9:7). In our day, there *are* still Saints throughout the world who are in need of help. Sometimes the most we can do for them is to fast and donate fast offerings. In other cases, our giving can be more direct and personal. Whatever forms our sacrifices take, it's worth examining our motivations for giving. Are our sacrifices expressions of love? After all, it's love that makes a giver cheerful.

 Ideas for Personal Scripture Study

2 CORINTHIANS 8:1–15; 9:5–15

I can cheerfully share what I have to bless the poor and needy.

There are so many people in need all over the world. How can we possibly make a difference? Elder Jeffrey R. Holland offered this counsel: "Rich *or* poor, we are to 'do what we can' when others are in need [see Mark 14:6, 8]. . . . [God] will help you and guide you in compassionate acts of discipleship if you are conscientiously wanting and praying and looking for ways to keep a commandment He has given us again and again" ("Are We Not All Beggars?," *Ensign* or *Liahona*, Nov. 2014, 41).

Read 2 Corinthians 8:1–15; 9:6–15, making note of principles Paul taught about caring for the poor and needy. What inspires you about Paul's counsel? You might pray for guidance about what you can do to bless someone in need. Be sure to record any impressions you receive and act on them.

See also Mosiah 4:16–27; Alma 34:27–29; Russell M. Nelson, "The Second Great Commandment," *Ensign* or *Liahona*, Nov. 2019, 96–100; Henry B. Eyring, "Is Not This the Fast That I Have Chosen?," *Ensign* or *Liahona*, May 2015, 22–25.

2 CORINTHIANS 11:1–6, 13–15; 13:5–9

"Examine yourselves, whether ye be in the faith."

Today, as in Paul's day, there are those who seek to lead us away "from the simplicity that is in Christ" (2 Corinthians 11:3). For that reason, it's crucial to do what Paul suggested: "Examine yourselves, whether ye be in the faith" (2 Corinthians 13:5). You could start this process by thinking about what it means to "be in the faith." How do you know if you are in the faith? Look for opportunities you have to examine yourself.

As part of your examination, you might also ponder the phrase "the simplicity that is in Christ" (2 Corinthians 11:3). How have you found simplicity in Christ and His gospel? How might your mind "be corrupted from [that] simplicity"? What helpful counsel do you find in 2 Corinthians 11:1–6, 13–15?

Consider also this counsel from President Dieter F. Uchtdorf: "If you ever think that the gospel isn't working so well for you, I invite you to step back, look at your life from a higher plane, and simplify your approach to discipleship. Focus on the basic doctrines, principles, and applications of the gospel. I promise that God will guide and bless you on your path to a fulfilling life, and the gospel will definitely work better for you" ("It Works Wonderfully!," *Ensign* or *Liahona*, Nov. 2015, 22).

2 CORINTHIANS 12:5–10

The Savior's grace is sufficient to help me find strength in my weakness.

We don't know what Paul's "thorn in the flesh" was, but we all have our own thorns that we wish God would remove from our lives. Think about your thorns as you read 2 Corinthians 12:5–10, and ponder what you learn about Jesus Christ in these verses. What did Paul teach in these verses about trials and weakness? What does it mean to you that God's "grace is sufficient" for you?

See also Mosiah 23:21–24; 24:10–15; Ether 12:27; Moroni 10:32–33.

 Ideas for Family Scripture Study and Home Evening

2 Corinthians 8–9. What do we find in these chapters that inspires us to reach out to the poor and others in need? This might be a good time to plan an act of service as a family for someone in need.

2 Corinthians 9:6–7. Does your family know someone who could be described as "a cheerful giver"? How can we make our service to others more cheerful? Younger family members could make badges that say "I am a cheerful giver." You could award the badges to family members whenever you see them serving one another cheerfully.

2 Corinthians 10:3–7. How could you teach your family about our "warfare" against wickedness? Would your family enjoy building a wall or a fort with chairs and blankets? This could lead to a discussion about how to cast down things that lead us away from God and how to "[bring] into captivity every thought to the obedience of Christ." What are the spiritual "weapons" we use to control our thoughts? (see Ephesians 6:11–18).

2 Corinthians 11:3. What can your family do to focus more on "the simplicity that is in Christ"?

For more ideas for teaching children, see this week's outline in *Come, Follow Me—For Primary*.

Suggested song: "'Give,' Said the Little Stream," *Children's Songbook*, 236.

Improving Personal Study

Record impressions. Elder Richard G. Scott said: "Knowledge carefully recorded is knowledge available in time of need. . . . [Recording spiritual direction] enhances the likelihood of your receiving further light" ("Acquiring Spiritual Knowledge," *Ensign*, Nov. 1993, 88; see also *Teaching in the Savior's Way*, 12, 30).

"Every man according as he purposeth in his heart, so let him give; not grudgingly, or of necessity: for God loveth a cheerful giver" (2 Corinthians 9:7).

Galatians

"WALK IN THE SPIRIT"

As you read Galatians, record the impressions you receive. Doing so will help you remember and ponder them in the future.

RECORD YOUR IMPRESSIONS

The gospel of Jesus Christ offers freedom from spiritual bondage. But sometimes people who have experienced the freedom of the gospel turn away from it and "desire again to be in bondage" (Galatians 4:9). This is what some Galatian Saints were doing—they were turning away from the liberty Christ had offered them (see Galatians 1:6). Paul's Epistle to the Galatians, then, was an urgent call to come back to "the liberty wherewith Christ hath made us free" (Galatians 5:1). This call is one we also need to hear and heed because while circumstances change, the struggle between freedom and bondage is constant. As Paul taught, it's not enough to be "called unto liberty" (Galatians 5:13); we must also "stand fast" in it (Galatians 5:1) by relying on Christ.

Ideas for Personal Scripture Study

The law of Christ makes me free.

Paul wrote to the Galatian Saints when he learned they were being led astray by false teachings (see Galatians 1:6–9). One of these teachings was that in order to be saved, Gentiles who had accepted the gospel needed to be circumcised and to keep other traditions of the law of Moses (see Galatians 2). Paul called these traditions the "yoke of bondage" (Galatians 5:1). As you read Paul's counsel to the Galatians, look for principles that can help you understand what true freedom is. You could also ponder what false traditions or other yokes of bondage might exist in your life. Is there anything that is preventing you from experiencing the freedom that the gospel offers? How have Christ and His gospel "made [you] free"? (Galatians 5:1).

See also 2 Nephi 2:27; 9:10–12.

GALATIANS 3

I am an heir to the blessings promised to Abraham.

Some of the Galatian Saints were concerned that because they were not literal descendants ("seed") of Abraham, they would not receive the blessings promised to Abraham, including exaltation. According to Galatians 3:7–9, 13–14, 27–29, what qualifies a person to be the "seed of Abraham"?

To learn about the blessings promised to Abraham and the blessings that we can inherit as his seed, see Gospel Topics, "Abrahamic Covenant" (topics.ChurchofJesusChrist.org). Why are the blessings promised to Abraham important to you?

GALATIANS 3:6–25

Abraham had the gospel of Jesus Christ.

The Prophet Joseph Smith explained: "We cannot believe that the ancients in all ages were so ignorant of the system of heaven as many suppose, since all that were ever saved, were saved through the power of this great plan of redemption, as much so before the coming of Christ as since. . . . Abraham offered sacrifice, and notwithstanding this, had the Gospel preached to him" ("The Elders of the Church in Kirtland to Their Brethren Abroad," *The Evening and the Morning Star*, Mar. 1834, 143, JosephSmithPapers.org). Why do you think it was important for the Saints in Paul's time to know that Abraham and other ancient prophets had the gospel of Jesus Christ? Why is it important to you to know this? (See Helaman 8:13–20; Moses 5:58–59; 6:50–66.)

See also *Teachings of Presidents of the Church: Joseph Smith* (2007), 45–56.

GALATIANS 5:13–26; 6:7–10

If I "walk in the Spirit," I will receive the "fruit of the Spirit."

Studying these verses can help you evaluate how fully you are walking in the Spirit. Are you experiencing the fruit of the Spirit mentioned in verses 22–23? What other fruit, or results, of spiritual living have you noticed? Ponder what you need to do to cultivate this fruit more fully. How might cultivating this fruit improve the important relationships in your life?

I must seek the "fruit of the Spirit" in my life.

If you are trying to walk in the Spirit but your efforts don't seem to be bearing the promised fruit, read Galatians 6:7–10. What message do you feel the Lord has for you in these verses?

See also Alma 32:28, 41–43; Doctrine and Covenants 64:32–34.

Ideas for Family Scripture Study and Home Evening

Galatians 3:11. What does it mean to "live by faith"? How are we living by faith as a family?

Galatians 4:1–7. You might introduce Galatians 4 by discussing the differences between a king's servants and his children. What opportunities or potential does a king's child have that a servant does not? Think about this as you read together verses 1–7. What do these verses teach about our relationship with Heavenly Father?

Galatians 5:16–26. Consider discussing the difference between the "works of the flesh" and the "fruit of the Spirit." To add some fun to your discussion, your family could label different fruits with words Paul used to describe the fruit of the Spirit. Then each family member could select one, define it, and talk about someone who exemplifies that fruit. This could lead to a discussion about ways your family could invite the Spirit into your home and cultivate this fruit. After the discussion, you could enjoy a fruit salad together.

Galatians 6:1–2. There may be times when someone in your family is "overtaken in a fault." What counsel do you find in Galatians 6:1–2 about what to do in such a situation?

Galatians 6:7–10. If your family has ever planted something together, you could use that experience to illustrate the principle "whatsoever a man soweth, that shall he also reap" (verse 7). Or you could ask family members about their favorite fruits or vegetables and talk about what it takes to grow a plant that produces that food. (See the picture at the end of this outline.) You could talk about the blessings your family hopes to receive and how to "reap" those blessings.

For more ideas for teaching children, see this week's outline in *Come, Follow Me—For Primary*.

Suggested song: "Teach Me to Walk in the Light," *Children's Songbook*, 177.

Improving Our Teaching

Help your family liken the scriptures to themselves. Nephi said, "I did liken all scriptures unto us, that it might be for our profit and learning" (1 Nephi 19:23). To help your family do this, you could invite them to ponder times when they have experienced the fruit of the Spirit described in Galatians 5:22–23. (See *Teaching in the Savior's Way*, 21.)

Paul taught that when we walk in the Spirit, we will experience the "fruit of the Spirit" in our lives.

Ephesians

"FOR THE PERFECTING OF THE SAINTS"

Do you see any connections between the messages in general conference and Paul's Epistle to the Ephesians?

RECORD YOUR IMPRESSIONS

When the gospel began to spread in Ephesus, it caused "no small stir" (Acts 19:23) among the Ephesians. Local craftsmen who produced shrines to a pagan goddess saw Christianity as a threat to their livelihood, and soon "they were full of wrath, . . . and the whole city was filled with confusion" (see Acts 19:27–29). Imagine being a new convert to the gospel in such a setting. Many Ephesians did accept and live the gospel amid this "uproar" (Acts 19:40), and Paul assured them that "Christ . . . is our peace" (Ephesians 2:13–14). These words, along with his invitation to "let all bitterness, and wrath, and anger, and clamour, and evil speaking, be put away" (Ephesians 4:31), seem as timely and comforting now as they were then. For the Ephesians, as for each of us, the strength to face adversity comes "in the Lord, and in the power of his might" (see Ephesians 6:10–13).

Ideas for Personal Scripture Study

EPHESIANS 1:4–11, 17–19

God chose, or foreordained, me to fulfill certain responsibilities on earth.

Paul spoke of the Saints being "predestinated" by God and "chosen . . . before the foundation of the world" to be His people. However, as President Henry B. Eyring has noted, this does not mean "that God must have determined in advance which of His children He would save and made the gospel available to them, while those who never heard the gospel simply were not 'chosen.' . . . God's plan is much more loving and just than that. Our Heavenly Father is anxious to gather and bless all of His family" ("Gathering the Family of God," *Ensign* or *Liahona*, May 2017, 20–21). All of God's children can accept the gospel and its ordinances because of the work performed for the dead in holy temples.

Although no one is predestined to be saved or not saved, modern revelation teaches that some of God's children were chosen, or "foreordained," in the premortal world to fulfill certain responsibilities in accomplishing God's purposes on earth. As you read Ephesians 1 and Gospel Topics, "Foreordination" (topics.ChurchofJesusChrist.org), ponder how this truth applies to you.

EPHESIANS 1:10

God will "gather together in one all things in Christ."

Why do you think our day is called "the dispensation of the fulness of times"? What might it mean to "gather together in one all things in Christ"? As you ponder these phrases, read the following scriptures: Ephesians 4:13; 2 Nephi 30:7–8; Doctrine and Covenants 110:11–16; 112:30–32; 128:18–21.

You may feel inspired to write your own explanations of these phrases.

See also David A. Bednar, "Gather Together in One All Things in Christ," *Ensign* or *Liahona*, Nov. 2018, 21–24.

EPHESIANS 2:19–22; 3:1–7; 4:11–16

The Church is founded on apostles and prophets, and Jesus Christ is the chief cornerstone.

According to Ephesians 2:19–22; 3:1–7; 4:11–16, why do we have prophets and apostles? Think about the messages from prophets and apostles you heard during general conference. How do their teachings fulfill the purposes Paul described? For example, how have these teachings helped you not be "carried about with every wind of doctrine"?

How is Jesus Christ like a cornerstone for the Church? How is He like a cornerstone for your life?

See also Acts 4:10–12.

Jesus Christ is the cornerstone of the Church.

EPHESIANS 5:21–6:4

Following the Savior's example can strengthen my family relationships.

As you read Ephesians 5:21–6:4, think about how the counsel in these verses could strengthen your family relationships.

It is important to note that Paul's words in Ephesians 5:22–24 were written in the context of the social customs of his era. Prophets and apostles today teach that men are not superior to women and that spouses are meant to be "equal partners" (see "The Family: A Proclamation to the World," ChurchofJesusChrist.org). Even so, you can still find relevant counsel in Ephesians 5:25–33. For example, how does Christ show His love for the Saints? What does this imply about how spouses, as equal partners, should treat each other? What messages do you find for yourself in these verses?

The armor of God will help protect me from evil.

As you read Ephesians 6:10–18, consider why Paul named each piece of armor the way he did. What does the "whole armour of God" protect you from? What can you do to more fully put on each piece of armor every day?

See also 2 Nephi 1:23; Doctrine and Covenants 27:15–18.

 # Ideas for Family Scripture Study and Home Evening

Ephesians 1:10. To teach about this verse, Elder David A. Bednar used the example of a rope (see "Gather Together in One All Things in Christ"). Consider showing family members a rope and letting them hold and examine it while you share parts of Elder Bednar's message. How is God gathering all things together in Christ? How are we blessed because of this gathering?

Ephesians 2:4–10; 3:14–21. Invite family members to share experiences in which they have felt the love and mercy of God and Jesus Christ described in these verses.

Ephesians 2:12–19. Your family might enjoy building walls out of pillows or other objects you have at home and then knocking them down. While Paul referred to the "wall" between Gentiles and Jews, what kinds of walls separate people today? How has Jesus Christ "broken down" these walls? How does He "reconcile [us] unto God"? (verse 16).

Ephesians 6:10–18. Your family could make their own "armour of God" using household items. The video "The Armour of God" (ChurchofJesusChrist.org) can help family members visualize this armor, and they can find simple explanations in "The Whole Armor of God" (*Friend*, June 2016, 24–25). How does each piece of armor protect us spiritually? What can we do to help each other "put on the whole armour of God" (Ephesians 6:11) every day?

For more ideas for teaching children, see this week's outline in *Come, Follow Me—For Primary*.

Suggested hymn: "Hope of Israel," *Hymns*, no. 259.

Improving Personal Study

Let the Spirit guide your study. Be sensitive to the Spirit as He guides you toward the things you need to learn each day, even if this leads you to study a topic that you hadn't originally planned.

Putting on the armor of God can protect us spiritually.

Philippians; Colossians

"I CAN DO ALL THINGS THROUGH CHRIST WHICH STRENGTHENETH ME"

When was the last time you read the spiritual impressions you have recorded during your study of the New Testament? It might be helpful to review the promptings you've been receiving.

RECORD YOUR IMPRESSIONS

Paul wrote his epistles to the Philippians and Colossians while he was a prisoner in Rome. But these letters don't have the tone you might expect from someone in prison. Paul spoke more about joy, rejoicing, and thanksgiving than he did about afflictions and trials: "Christ is preached," he said, "and I therein do rejoice, yea, and will rejoice" (Philippians 1:18). And "though I be absent in the flesh, yet am I with you in the spirit, joying and beholding . . . the steadfastness of your faith in Christ" (Colossians 2:5). Certainly, "the peace of God" that Paul experienced in his difficult circumstances "passeth all understanding" (Philippians 4:7), but it was nonetheless a reality. In our own trials, we can feel this same peace and "rejoice in the Lord alway" (Philippians 4:4). We can, as Paul did, rely completely upon Jesus Christ, "in whom we have redemption" (Colossians 1:14). We can say, as did Paul, "I can do all things through Christ which strengtheneth me" (Philippians 4:13; see also Colossians 1:11).

 Ideas for Personal Scripture Study

PHILIPPIANS 2:5–11; COLOSSIANS 1:12–23

My faith is founded on Jesus Christ.

President Russell M. Nelson said that when he focused his scripture study on verses about Jesus Christ, it had such an impact on him that he felt like "a different man!" ("Drawing the

Power of Jesus Christ into Our Lives," *Ensign* or *Liahona*, May 2017, 39). Consider following his example as you read Philippians and Colossians (see especially Philippians 2:5–11; Colossians 1:12–23). What do you learn about the Savior? How can these truths help you become "a different man" or woman?

PHILIPPIANS 2:12–13

Do we "work out [our] own salvation"?

Some people use the phrase "work out your own salvation" (Philippians 2:12) to support the idea that we are saved only by our own efforts. Others use Paul's teaching "by grace are ye saved through faith" (Ephesians 2:8) to claim that no works are required for salvation. However, the scriptures, including the writings of Paul, clearly teach the need for both the grace of Jesus Christ and personal effort in order to receive salvation. And even in our best efforts to work out our salvation, "it is God which worketh in you" (Philippians 2:13; see also Philippians 1:6; 2 Nephi 25:23; Bible Dictionary, "Grace").

PHILIPPIANS 3:4–14

The gospel of Jesus Christ is worth every sacrifice.

Paul gave up much when he converted to the gospel of Jesus Christ, including the influential place he held in Jewish society as a Pharisee. In Philippians 3:4–14, look for what Paul gained because he was willing to make sacrifices for the gospel. How did he feel about his sacrifices?

Then consider your own discipleship. What have you sacrificed for the gospel of Jesus Christ? What have you received? Are there any additional sacrifices you feel you need to make to become a more dedicated disciple of the Savior?

See also 3 Nephi 9:19–20; Doctrine and Covenants 58:2–5; Taylor G. Godoy, "One More Day," *Ensign* or *Liahona*, May 2018, 34–36.

PHILIPPIANS 4:1–13

I can find joy in Christ, regardless of my circumstances.

Paul's life is a vivid illustration of the truth expressed by President Russell M. Nelson: "When the focus of our lives is on . . . Jesus Christ and His gospel, we can feel joy regardless of what is happening—or not happening—in our lives. Joy comes from and because of Him" ("Joy and Spiritual Survival," *Ensign* or *Liahona*, Nov. 2016, 82).

As you read Philippians—particularly chapter 4—search for statements that can help you find joy in any circumstance of your life. When have you experienced "the peace of God" during a challenging time? (verse 7). When have you found strength "through Christ" to do hard things? (verse 13). Why do you think it is important to "be content" in all circumstances? (verse 11). How can practicing the attributes in verse 8 help you find joy in your circumstances?

See Alma 33:23; Dieter F. Uchtdorf, "Grateful in Any Circumstances," *Ensign* or *Liahona*, May 2014, 70–77.

COLOSSIANS 3:1–17

Disciples of Jesus Christ become "new" as they live His gospel.

How can you tell that Jesus Christ is helping you become a "new man [or woman]"? One way to ponder this is to explore Colossians 3:1–17 and make a list of the attitudes, attributes, and actions of the "old man" and another list of the attitudes, attributes, and actions of the "new man."

Record your thoughts about how the Savior is changing you, so that you can review them in the future and ponder how you are progressing.

 ## Ideas for Family Scripture Study and Home Evening

Philippians. Your family may notice the words *joy* or *rejoice* repeated often in Philippians. Each time you come across one of these words, you could stop and discuss what Paul taught about how to find joy.

Philippians 2:14–16. How can we "shine as lights in the world"?

Philippians 4:8. Family members could identify things to "think on" that fit the descriptions in this verse (see also Articles of Faith 1:13). How would your family be blessed by following Paul's counsel?

Colossians 1:23; 2:7. Perhaps your family could read these verses while sitting around a tree or looking at a picture of a tree (such as the one that accompanies this outline). What does it mean to be "grounded" and "rooted" in Christ? How can we help each other strengthen our spiritual roots?

Colossians 2:2–3. Your family might enjoy filling a "treasure chest" with things that represent the "riches" and "treasures of wisdom and knowledge" you find in the gospel.

For more ideas for teaching children, see this week's outline in *Come, Follow Me—For Primary.*

Suggested hymn: "Rejoice, the Lord Is King!," *Hymns*, no. 66.

Improving Our Teaching

Live your testimony. "You teach what you are," Elder Neal A. Maxwell taught. "Your traits will be more remembered . . . than a particular truth in a particular lesson" (in *Teaching in the Savior's Way*, 13).

Paul taught that our faith should be "rooted" in Jesus Christ (Colossians 2:7).

1 and 2 Thessalonians

"PERFECT THAT WHICH IS LACKING IN YOUR FAITH"

If we do not record the impressions we receive from the Spirit, we might forget them. What does the Spirit prompt you to record as you read 1 and 2 Thessalonians?

RECORD YOUR IMPRESSIONS

In Thessalonica, Paul and Silas were accused of having "turned the world upside down" (Acts 17:6). Their preaching angered certain leaders among the Jews, and these leaders stirred the people into an uproar (see Acts 17:1–10). As a result, Paul and Silas were advised to leave Thessalonica. Paul worried about the new Thessalonian converts and the persecution they were facing, but he was unable to return to visit them. "When I could no longer forbear," he wrote, "I sent to know your faith." In response, Paul's assistant Timothy, who had been serving in Thessalonica, "brought us good tidings of your faith and charity" (1 Thessalonians 3:5–6). In fact, the Thessalonian Saints were known as examples "to all that believe" (1 Thessalonians 1:7), and news of their faith spread to cities abroad. Imagine Paul's joy and relief to hear that his work among them "was not in vain" (1 Thessalonians 2:1). But Paul knew that faithfulness in the past is not sufficient for spiritual survival in the future, and he was wary of the influence of false teachers among the Saints (see 2 Thessalonians 2:2–3). His message to them, and to us, is to continue to "perfect that which is lacking in [our] faith" and to "increase more and more" in love (see 1 Thessalonians 3:10; 4:10).

 ## Ideas for Personal Scripture Study

1 THESSALONIANS 1–2

Disciples of Christ serve others with sincerity and love.

In 1 Thessalonians, Paul's words reveal both the concern and the joy of someone who has given himself wholly to serving God's children. Especially in the first two chapters of 1 Thessalonians, you will find words and phrases that describe the attitudes and actions of a disciple of the Lord. For example, what do you learn from 1 Thessalonians 1:5–8; 2:1–13 about serving the Lord?

Think about your own opportunities to serve God and His children. What do you find in these chapters that inspires you to improve your service? Consider asking yourself questions based on what you find, such as "Am I an example of the things I know?" (see 1 Thessalonians 1:7).

1 THESSALONIANS 3:7–13; 4:1–12

"Increase and abound in love."

Paul rejoiced in the faithfulness of the Thessalonian Saints (see 1 Thessalonians 3:7–9). But he also wanted them to "abound more and more" in that faithfulness (1 Thessalonians 4:1). As you read 1 Thessalonians 3:7–13; 4:1–12, ponder ways you can "increase more and more" spiritually (1 Thessalonians 4:10). For example, notice that Paul used words like "holiness" and "sanctification." What do you learn from Paul's writings about the meanings of these words? How can the Savior help you become more holy and sanctified?

See also Guide to the Scriptures, "Holy," "Sanctification," scriptures.ChurchofJesusChrist.org.

1 THESSALONIANS 4:16–18; 5:1–10; 2 THESSALONIANS 1:4–10

If I am faithful and watchful, I will be prepared for the Savior's Second Coming.

In 1 Thessalonians 5:1–10, Paul used several metaphors to teach about the time when Jesus will return to the earth. As you study these metaphors, consider writing down the impressions that come to you about the Second Coming of Jesus Christ:

- "A thief in the night":____

- "Travail upon a woman with child":____________________________

- Other metaphors you find:_____________________________________

What additional truths do you learn from 1 Thessalonians 4:16–18; 5:1–10; 2 Thessalonians 1:4–10? What are you prompted to do to watch and prepare for the Savior's coming?

See also D. Todd Christofferson, "Preparing for the Lord's Return," *Ensign* or *Liahona*, May 2019, 81–84.

2 THESSALONIANS 2

An apostasy, or falling away from truth, was prophesied to precede the Second Coming.

Amid increasing persecutions, many Thessalonian Saints believed the Savior's Second Coming must be near. But Paul knew that before Jesus returned to earth there would be an apostasy—a rebellion or "falling away" from the truth (see 2 Thessalonians 2:1–4). You could deepen your understanding of the Great Apostasy—and your appreciation for the Restoration—by pondering some of the following:

- *Scriptures that foretold the Apostasy:* Isaiah 24:5; Amos 8:11–12; Matthew 24:4–14; 2 Timothy 4:3–4

- *Scriptures that show the Apostasy was already beginning in Paul's time:* Acts 20:28–30; Galatians 1:6–7; 1 Timothy 1:5–7

- *Observations about the Great Apostasy by Christian reformers:*

Martin Luther: "I have sought nothing beyond reforming the Church in conformity with the Holy Scriptures. . . . I simply say that Christianity has ceased to exist among those who should have preserved it" (in E. G. Schweibert, *Luther and His Times: The Reformation from a New Perspective* [1950], 590).

Roger Williams: "The apostasy . . . hath so far corrupted all that there can be no recovery out of that apostasy till Christ send forth new apostles to plant churches anew" (in Philip Schaff, *The Creeds of Christendom* [1877], 851).

See also 2 Nephi 28; Gospel Topics, "Apostasy," topics.ChurchofJesusChrist.org.

 ## Ideas for Family Scripture Study and Home Evening

1 Thessalonians 3:9–13. What impresses you about the feelings Paul had for his friends? How can we "increase and abound in love one toward another"? (verse 12).

1 Thessalonians 4:13–18. What phrases in these verses about the Resurrection give you comfort?

1 Thessalonians 5:14–25. As you review Paul's counsel in 1 Thessalonians 5:14–25, invite each family member to find a phrase that the family could focus on. Find creative ways to display these phrases in your home as a reminder. For example, each person might find or draw pictures that illustrate or reinforce the phrase he or she chose.

2 Thessalonians 3:13. Do we ever feel "weary in well doing"—overwhelmed, perhaps, with the demands of discipleship? What helps us when we feel this way? (See Galatians 6:9; Doctrine and Covenants 64:33.) How can we support each other when this happens?

For more ideas for teaching children, see this week's outline in *Come, Follow Me—For Primary.*

Suggested song: "I'm Trying to Be like Jesus," *Children's Songbook,* 78–79.

Improving Personal Study

Seek revelation daily. "Revelation often comes 'line upon line' (2 Nephi 28:30), not all at once. . . . Don't think of [gospel study] as something you make time for but as something you are always doing" (*Teaching in the Savior's Way,* 12).

Resurrected Christ, by Robert T. Barrett

1 and 2 Timothy; Titus; Philemon

"BE THOU AN EXAMPLE OF THE BELIEVERS"

Sometimes it's helpful to approach your scripture study with one or more questions in mind. Invite the Spirit to guide you to answers as you study, and record any inspiration you receive.

RECORD YOUR IMPRESSIONS

In the epistles Paul wrote to Timothy, Titus, and Philemon, we get a glimpse into the heart of a servant of the Lord. Unlike Paul's other epistles to entire congregations, these were written to individuals—Paul's close friends and associates in God's work—and reading them is like listening in on a conversation. We see Paul encouraging Timothy and Titus, two leaders of congregations, in their Church service. We see him entreating his friend Philemon to reconcile with a fellow Saint and treat him like a brother in the gospel. Paul's words were not addressed to us directly, and he may never have expected that so many people would one day read them. Yet we find in these epistles counsel and encouragement for us, whatever our personal ministry in the service of Christ might be.

 Ideas for Personal Scripture Study

Who were Timothy and Titus?

Timothy and Titus had served with Paul on some of his missionary journeys. During their service, they earned Paul's respect and trust. Timothy was later called as a Church leader in Ephesus, and Titus was called as a leader in Crete. In these epistles, Paul gave Timothy and Titus instruction and encouragement regarding their responsibilities, which included preaching the gospel and calling men to serve as bishops.

See also Bible Dictionary, "Pauline Epistles," "Timothy," "Titus."

"Let no man despise thy youth; but be thou an example of the believers" (1 Timothy 4:12).

"Be thou an example of the believers."

Timothy was relatively young, but Paul knew that he could be a great Church leader despite his youth. What counsel did Paul give to Timothy in 1 Timothy 4:10–16? How can this counsel help you lead others to the Savior and His gospel?

See also Alma 17:11.

"God hath not given us the spirit of fear; but of power, and of love, and of a sound mind."

2 Timothy is believed to be the last epistle Paul wrote, and it seems that he knew his time on earth was short (see 2 Timothy 4:6–8). How might Timothy have felt, knowing that he might soon be without his trusted mentor and leader? What did Paul say to encourage him? You might also read with your own challenges and fears in mind. What messages of hope and encouragement does the Lord have for you in 2 Timothy?

See also Kelly R. Johnson, "Enduring Power," *Ensign* or *Liahona*, Nov. 2020, 112–14.

Living the gospel provides safety from the spiritual dangers of the last days.

We are living in "the last days" that Paul spoke of, and the "perilous times" have come (2 Timothy 3:1). As you read 2 Timothy 3, write down the perils of the last days that are mentioned (see also 1 Timothy 4:1–3):

____

____

____

____

Can you think of examples of these perils in the world around you—or in your own life? How do these perils, like the people described in verse 6, "creep into [your house], and lead [you] captive"? What counsel do you find in 2 Timothy 3, and elsewhere in these epistles, that could keep you and your family safe from these spiritual dangers? (see, for example, 1 Timothy 1:3–11; 2 Timothy 2:15–16; Titus 2:1–8).

Who was Philemon?

Philemon was a Christian who had been converted to the gospel by Paul. Philemon owned a slave named Onesimus, who apparently escaped to Rome. There Onesimus met Paul and converted to the gospel. Paul sent Onesimus back to Philemon with a letter encouraging Philemon to receive Onesimus "not now as a servant, but above a servant, a brother beloved" (Philemon 1:16).

Disciples of Jesus Christ treat one another like brothers and sisters.

As you read Paul's epistle to Philemon, ponder how you might apply his counsel to your relationships with others. Below are some questions you could consider:

- Verses 1–7: What do words like "fellowlabourer" and "fellowsoldier" suggest to you about relationships among Saints? When have you felt "refreshed by" a brother or sister in Christ?

- Verses 8–16: What does it mean to "enjoin" and "beseech"? Why did Paul choose to *beseech* Philemon rather than *enjoin* him? What did Paul hope would be accomplished by sending Onesimus back to Philemon?

- Verse 16: What does it mean to be "a brother [or sister] beloved . . . in the Lord"? Do you know someone who you need to receive in this way?

 ## Ideas for Family Scripture Study and Home Evening

1 Timothy 2:9–10. What does it mean to "adorn [ourselves] . . . with good works"? What are some good works our family could do this week? You might sing together a song about doing good, such as "Have I Done Any Good?" (*Hymns*, no. 223).

1 Timothy 4:12. To help your family members desire to be "an example of the believers," consider inviting them to draw pictures of people who have been good examples to them. How have these people inspired us to follow Jesus Christ? President Thomas S. Monson's message "Be an Example and a Light" (*Ensign* or *Liahona*, Nov. 2015, 86–88) can give some ideas on how to be an example to others.

1 Timothy 6:7–12. Why do you think "the love of money is the root of all evil"? What are the dangers of focusing our lives on money or possessions? How can we be content with the blessings we have?

2 Timothy 3:14–17. According to these verses, what blessings come to those who know and study the scriptures? Perhaps family members could share scriptures they have found to be especially "profitable."

Philemon 1:17–21. What was Paul willing to do for Onesimus? How is this similar to what the Savior willingly did for us? (see also 1 Timothy 2:5–6; Doctrine and Covenants 45:3–5). How can we follow the examples of Paul and the Savior?

For more ideas for teaching children, see this week's outline in *Come, Follow Me—For Primary*.

Suggested song: "Shine On," *Children's Songbook*, 144.

Improving Our Teaching

Teach clear and simple doctrine. The gospel is beautiful in its simplicity (see Doctrine and Covenants 133:57). Rather than trying to entertain your family with lessons requiring much preparation, strive to teach pure and simple doctrine (see 1 Timothy 1:3–7).

"From a child thou hast known the holy scriptures, which are able to make thee wise unto salvation through faith which is in Christ Jesus" (2 Timothy 3:15).

Hebrews 1–6

JESUS CHRIST, "THE AUTHOR OF ETERNAL SALVATION"

Recording spiritual impressions helps you recognize what the Holy Ghost wants to teach you. Acting on your impressions demonstrates your faith that those promptings are real.

RECORD YOUR IMPRESSIONS

Each of us has to give up something in order to accept the gospel of Jesus Christ—bad habits, incorrect beliefs, unwholesome associations, or something else. For Gentiles in the early Christian Church, conversion often meant abandoning false gods. For the Hebrews (or Jews), conversion proved to be, if not more difficult, a little more complicated. After all, their cherished beliefs and traditions were rooted in the worship of the true God and the teachings of His prophets, extending back thousands of years. Yet the Apostles taught that the law of Moses had been fulfilled in Jesus Christ and that a higher law was now the standard for believers. Would accepting Christianity mean that the Hebrews must give up their earlier beliefs and history? The Epistle to the Hebrews sought to help settle such questions by teaching that the law of Moses, the prophets, and the ordinances are all important, but Jesus Christ is greater (see Hebrews 1:1–4; 3:1–6; 7:23–28). In fact, all these things point to and testify of Christ as the Son of God and the promised Messiah the Jews had been waiting for.

Conversion, in those early days and today, means making Jesus Christ the center of our worship and our lives. It means holding fast to truth and letting go of that which distracts us from Him, for He is the "author of eternal salvation unto all them that obey him" (Hebrews 5:9).

 Ideas for Personal Scripture Study

Who wrote the Epistle to the Hebrews?

Some scholars have questioned whether Paul wrote the Epistle to the Hebrews. The literary style of Hebrews is somewhat different from Paul's other letters, and the earliest versions of the text did not name an author. However, because the ideas expressed in Hebrews are consistent with Paul's other teachings, Latter-day Saints, in keeping with Christian tradition, have generally accepted that Paul was at least involved in writing this epistle.

See also Bible Dictionary, "Pauline Epistles."

HEBREWS 1–5

Jesus Christ is "the express image" of Heavenly Father.

Many Jews found it difficult to accept Jesus Christ as the Son of God. Notice how the Epistle to the Hebrews testifies of Him. For example, as you read the first five chapters, you might make a list of Jesus Christ's titles, roles, attributes, and works that you find mentioned. What do these things teach you about the Savior? What do they teach you about Heavenly Father?

What does the following statement from Elder Jeffrey R. Holland add to your understanding of the teachings in these chapters? "Jesus . . . came to improve man's view of God and to plead with them to love their Heavenly Father as He has always and will always love them. . . . So feeding the hungry, healing the sick, rebuking hypocrisy, pleading for faith—this was Christ showing us the way of the Father" ("The Grandeur of God," *Ensign* or *Liahona*, Nov. 2003, 72).

HEBREWS 2:9–18; 4:12–16; 5:7–8

Jesus Christ suffered all things so that He can understand and help me when I suffer.

Do you feel that you can "come boldly unto the throne of grace" and seek mercy? (Hebrews 4:16). One message of the Epistle to the Hebrews is that despite our sins and weaknesses, God is approachable and His grace is attainable. What do you find in Hebrews 2:9–18; 4:12–16; 5:7–8 that strengthens your confidence that Jesus Christ will help you with your mortal challenges? Consider recording in a journal your thoughts and feelings about what the Savior has done for you.

See also Mosiah 3:7–11; Alma 7:11–13; 34; Matthew S. Holland, "The Exquisite Gift of the Son," *Ensign* or *Liahona*, Nov. 2020, 45–47.

HEBREWS 3:7–4:11

God's blessings are available to those who "harden not [their] hearts."

By retelling the story of the ancient Israelites, Paul hoped to persuade the Jews to avoid the mistake their ancestors made—rejecting God's blessings because of unbelief. (You can read the story Paul alluded to in Numbers 14:1–12, 26–35.)

Consider how Hebrews 3:7–4:11 might apply to you. To do this, you might ponder questions like these:

- How did the Israelites provoke the Lord? (see Hebrews 3:8–11). What are the consequences of having a hard heart?

- When have I allowed my heart to become hardened? Are there any blessings God wants to give me that I am not receiving because of a lack of faith?

- What can I do to develop a soft and contrite heart? (see Ether 4:15; Proverbs 3:5–6; Alma 5:14–15).

See also 1 Nephi 2:16; 15:6–11; Jacob 1:7–8; Alma 12:33–36; Neill F. Marriott, "Yielding Our Hearts to God," *Ensign* or *Liahona*, Nov. 2015, 30–32.

 ## Ideas for Family Scripture Study and Home Evening

Hebrews 1:8–9. In what ways has Jesus shown that He loves righteousness and hates iniquity? If we have unrighteous desires, what can we do to change them?

Hebrews 2:1–4. Can you think of an object lesson to help your family understand what it means to keep a firm hold on the gospel truths "which we have heard"? You might illustrate this with an object that is hard to hold onto. How are our efforts to maintain our testimony like catching and holding this object? How can we make sure "the things which we have heard" do not "slip" away from us? (verse 1).

Hebrews 2:9–10. To explore the phrase "captain of their salvation," you could begin by discussing what a captain does. What does salvation mean? How is Jesus Christ like a captain for us and our salvation?

Hebrews 5:1–5. These verses can help you have a discussion about what it means to be called of God by someone who has authority. What can we learn from the example of Jesus Christ about receiving and fulfilling callings?

"No man taketh this honour unto himself, but he that is called of God, as was Aaron" (Hebrews 5:4). *Moses Calls Aaron to the Ministry*, by Harry Anderson

For more ideas for teaching children, see this week's outline in *Come, Follow Me—For Primary*.

Suggested hymn: "I Need Thee Every Hour," *Hymns*, no. 98.

Improving Personal Study

Try different approaches. Instead of always studying the scriptures in the same way, consider various study ideas. For some ideas, see "Ideas to Improve Your Personal Scripture Study" at the beginning of this resource.

Light of the World, by Walter Rane

Hebrews 7–13

"AN HIGH PRIEST OF GOOD THINGS TO COME"

As you read Hebrews 7–13, you may receive impressions through the Holy Ghost. Consider ways you can record them; for example, you could record them in this outline, in the margins of your scriptures, or in a notebook or journal.

RECORD YOUR IMPRESSIONS

Even faithful Saints at times suffer "reproaches and afflictions" that can shake their confidence (see Hebrews 10:32–38). Paul knew that Jewish converts to Christianity were experiencing severe persecution because of their new faith. To encourage them to stay true to their testimonies, he reminded them of the long tradition of faithful believers from their own history: Abel, Enoch, Noah, Abraham, Sara, Joseph, Moses—"a cloud of witnesses" that God's promises are real and worth waiting for (see Hebrews 11; 12:1). This tradition is yours too. It's a heritage of faith shared by all those who look "unto Jesus [as] the author and finisher of our faith" (Hebrews 12:2). Because of Him, whenever adversity makes us want to "draw back," we can instead "draw near with a true heart in full assurance of faith" (Hebrews 10:22, 38). For us, as for the ancient Saints, Jesus Christ is our "high priest of good things to come" (Hebrews 9:11).

 Ideas for Personal Scripture Study

The Melchizedek Priesthood points me to Jesus Christ.

For centuries, the Jews had exercised the Levitical Priesthood, also known as the Aaronic Priesthood. But with the fulness of the gospel of Jesus Christ came the restoration of the greater Melchizedek Priesthood, which offered even greater blessings. What do you learn about the

Melchizedek Priesthood from Hebrews 7? Keeping in mind that the purpose of this epistle—like all scripture—is to build faith in Jesus Christ, you might note passages that testify of Him.

Here are some examples of other truths you might find:

- **Joseph Smith Translation, Hebrews 7:3, 21:** Those who are ordained to the Melchizedek Priesthood "are made like unto the Son of God" and are "[priests] forever."

- **Hebrews 7:11:** The Levitical Priesthood does not offer "perfection" and was therefore superseded by the Melchizedek (see Doctrine and Covenants 84:18–22).

- **Hebrews 7:20–21:** The Melchizedek Priesthood is received through an "oath and covenant" (see Doctrine and Covenants 84:33–44).

What blessings have you received from the Melchizedek Priesthood and "the ordinances thereof"? (Doctrine and Covenants 84:20). How has the Melchizedek Priesthood helped you come unto Christ?

See also Alma 13:1–13; Doctrine and Covenants 121:36–46; Gospel Topics, "Melchizedek Priesthood," topics.ChurchofJesusChrist.org; Guide to the Scriptures, "Melchizedek," scriptures.ChurchofJesusChrist.org; Russell M. Nelson, "Spiritual Treasures," *Ensign* or *Liahona*, Nov. 2019, 76–79; Dallin H. Oaks, "The Melchizedek Priesthood and the Keys," *Ensign* or *Liahona*, May 2020, 69–72.

HEBREWS 9; 10:1–22

Ancient and modern ordinances point to Jesus Christ.

The original Hebrew readers of this epistle would have been very familiar with the ancient tabernacle and the ordinances Paul described. But some did not fully recognize that the purpose of these ordinances was to point to the atoning sacrifice of Jesus Christ.

In biblical times, on a yearly holiday called the Day of Atonement, a high priest entered the holiest place (or Holy of Holies) in the Jerusalem temple and sacrificed a goat or lamb to atone for the sins of Israel.

As you read Paul's description of these ordinances, look for symbols and teachings that help you better understand the Savior's atoning mission.

The ordinances we participate in today are different from those in Paul's time, but their purpose is the same. How do today's ordinances testify to you of Jesus Christ?

To learn more about ancient Jewish ceremonies and their symbolism, see the videos "The Tabernacle" and "Sacrifice and Sacrament" (ChurchofJesusChrist.org).

HEBREWS 11

Faith requires trusting in God's promises.

If someone asked you to define faith, what would you say? Sister Anne C. Pingree drew on language from Hebrews 11 to give this definition of faith: "The spiritual ability to be persuaded of promises that are seen 'afar off' but that may not be attained in this life" ("Seeing the Promises Afar Off," *Ensign* or *Liahona*, Nov. 2003, 14).

Consider developing your own definition of faith as you ponder the ideas in Hebrews 11. What do the examples of the people mentioned in this chapter teach you about faith? (See also Ether 12:6–22.)

What promises do you see "afar off"? How can you show the Lord that you are "persuaded of them, and [have] embraced them"? (Hebrews 11:13).

See also Alma 32:21, 26–43; Jeffrey R. Holland, "An High Priest of Good Things to Come," *Ensign*, Nov. 1999, 36–38; Gospel Topics, "Faith in Jesus Christ," topics.ChurchofJesusChrist.org.

 ## Ideas for Family Scripture Study and Home Evening

Hebrews 10:32–36. You might invite family members to share spiritual experiences when they felt "illuminated" with truth. How can these experiences help us "cast not away therefore [our] confidence" in times of trial or doubt?

Hebrews 11. How can you help your family members learn from the faithful examples mentioned in Hebrews 11? It might be fun to act out the stories of some of these examples. You can review some of these stories in *Old Testament Stories*. Or perhaps your family could discuss the examples of other faithful people you know—including ancestors, Church leaders, and members of your community. You could also sing a song about faith, such as "Faith" (*Children's Songbook*, 96–97).

Hebrews 12:2. According to this verse, why was Jesus willing to endure the pain and suffering of the cross? What does this teach us about how we can endure our trials? President Russell M. Nelson gave some helpful insights on this verse in his message "Joy and Spiritual Survival" (*Ensign* or *Liahona*, Nov. 2016, 81–84).

Hebrews 12:5–11. Why does the Lord chasten and correct us? What do we notice in these verses about the way the Lord sees chastisement? How do these verses affect the way we give or receive chastisement?

For more ideas for teaching children, see this week's outline in *Come, Follow Me—For Primary*.

Suggested song: "Faith," *Children's Songbook*, 96–97.

Improving Our Teaching

Use music to invite the Spirit and learn doctrine. The First Presidency said, "Music has boundless powers for moving [us] toward greater spirituality" ("First Presidency Preface," *Hymns*, x). Perhaps a song about faith, such as "True to the Faith" (*Hymns*, no. 254), would supplement a family discussion from Hebrews 11.

The symbols and ordinances of the ancient temple taught about the role of Jesus Christ.

James

"BE YE DOERS OF THE WORD, AND NOT HEARERS ONLY"

As you read the Epistle of James, pay attention to phrases that stand out to you. How are you prompted to be a "doer" of these words? (James 1:22).

RECORD YOUR IMPRESSIONS

Sometimes just one verse of scripture can change the world. James 1:5 seems like a simple bit of counsel—if you need wisdom, ask God. But when 14-year-old Joseph Smith read that verse, "it seemed to enter with great force into every feeling of [his] heart" (Joseph Smith—History 1:12). Thus inspired, Joseph acted on James's admonition and sought wisdom from God through prayer. And God did indeed give liberally, giving Joseph one of the most remarkable heavenly visitations in human history—the First Vision. This vision changed the course of Joseph's life and led to the Restoration of the Church of Jesus Christ on the earth. All of us are blessed today because Joseph Smith read and acted on James 1:5.

What will you find as you study the Epistle of James? Perhaps a verse or two will change you or someone you love. You may find guidance as you seek to fulfill your mission in life. You may find encouragement to speak kindly or to be more patient. You may feel prompted to make your actions align better with your faith. Whatever inspires you, let these words "enter . . . into every feeling of [your] heart." And then, when you "receive with meekness the . . . word," as James wrote, be a doer of the word, not a hearer only (see James 1:21–22).

Ideas for Personal Scripture Study

Who was James?

It is generally believed that the author of the Epistle of James was a son of Mary, the mother of Jesus Christ, and therefore the half brother of the Savior. James is mentioned in Matthew 13:55; Mark 6:3; Acts 12:17; 15:13; 21:18; and Galatians 1:19; 2:9. It appears from these scriptures that James was a Church leader in Jerusalem and had been called as an Apostle (see Galatians 1:19).

JAMES 1:2–4; 5:7–11

Patient endurance leads to perfection.

After reading James 1:2–4; 5:7–11, what would you say was James's main message about patience? It might help to ponder what Elder Jeremy R. Jaggi's family learned about patience from these verses (see "Let Patience Have Her Perfect Work, and Count It All Joy!," *Ensign* or *Liahona*, Nov. 2020, 99–101). What is the "perfect work" of patience? (James 1:4). How can you show the Lord that you are willing to be patient?

JAMES 1:3–8, 21–25; 2:14–26; 4:17

Faith requires action.

How do you know if you have faith in Jesus Christ? How do your works demonstrate your faith in God? Think about these questions as you study James's teachings about faith. It might be interesting to also read about Abraham and Rahab, two examples James mentioned (see Genesis 22:1–12; Joshua 2). How did they show that they had faith in God?

Reading James 1:3–8, 21–25; 2:14–26; 4:17 may help you think of ways you could be a better doer of the word. Record any impressions you receive, and make plans to act on them.

See also Alma 34:27–29; 3 Nephi 27:21.

"Abraham believed God, and it was imputed unto him for righteousness" (James 2:23). *Abraham on the Plains of Mamre,* by Grant Romney Clawson

JAMES 1:26; 3:1–18

The words I speak have the power to hurt or bless others.

Among the rich imagery James used throughout his epistle, some of his most vivid language is found in his counsel *about* language. Consider making a list of all the ways James described the tongue or mouth. What does each comparison or image suggest about the words we speak? Think of something you can do to bless someone with your words (see Doctrine and Covenants 108:7).

As a disciple of Jesus Christ, I should love all people, regardless of their circumstances.

James warned the Saints specifically against favoring the rich and despising the poor, but his warning can apply to any biases or prejudices we may have toward others. As you prayerfully study James 2:1–9, search your own heart and listen for the Holy Ghost's promptings. It might help to replace phrases in these verses, such as "a poor man in vile raiment" (verse 2), with other words or phrases that describe someone you might be tempted to judge unfairly. Do you sense any changes you need to make in the way you treat or think of others?

Ideas for Family Scripture Study and Home Evening

James 1:5. After reading James 1:5, your family could summarize the account of the First Vision (see Joseph Smith—History 1:8–20) or watch the video "Ask of God: Joseph Smith's First Vision" (ChurchofJesusChrist.org). Invite family members to share their testimonies of the Prophet Joseph Smith and experiences when Heavenly Father answered their prayers.

James 1:26–27. Consider watching the video "True Christianity" (ChurchofJesusChrist.org). Then read James's definition of "pure religion" in James 1:26–27, and discuss ways your family can make your practice of religion more pure.

James 3. James 3 includes many images that could inspire memorable object lessons to help your family remember to speak kindly. For example, you could build a fire together and talk about how a small, unkind word can cause a big problem (see verses 5–6). Or you could serve something sour in something that is usually used for sweet food—such as lemon juice in a honey jar. This could lead to a discussion about using sweet and uplifting words (see verses 9–14).

James 4:5–8. Why should we "draw nigh to God" (James 4:8) when we face temptation?

James 5:14–16. President Dallin H. Oaks taught that "parents should encourage more priesthood blessings in the family" ("The Powers of the Priesthood," *Ensign* or *Liahona*, May 2018, 67). Perhaps reading James 5:14–16 and sharing experiences about receiving a priesthood blessing could encourage family members to ask for a blessing when they are sick or need spiritual strength.

For more ideas for teaching children, see this week's outline in *Come, Follow Me—For Primary*.

Suggested hymn: "Have I Done Any Good?," *Hymns*, no. 223.

Improving Personal Study

Act on what you learn. As you study, listen to promptings from the Spirit about how you can apply what you are learning to your life. Commit to follow these promptings and live the gospel more fully. (See *Teaching in the Savior's Way*, 35.)

James's admonition to "ask of God" (James 1:5) inspired Joseph Smith to seek wisdom from God. Photograph by Christina Smith.

1 and 2 Peter

"REJOICE WITH JOY UNSPEAKABLE AND FULL OF GLORY"

As you read the Epistles of Peter, you may receive spiritual impressions. Promptly record them while you are "yet in the Spirit" (Doctrine and Covenants 76:80) so you can accurately capture what God teaches you.

RECORD YOUR IMPRESSIONS

Shortly after His Resurrection, the Savior made a prophecy that must have been troubling to Peter. He foretold that Peter would be martyred for his faith, being carried "whither [he] wouldest not . . . , signifying by what death he should glorify God" (John 21:18–19). Years later, when Peter wrote his epistles, he knew that his prophesied martyrdom was near: "Shortly I must put off this my tabernacle, even as our Lord Jesus Christ hath shewed me" (2 Peter 1:14). And yet Peter's words were not filled with fear or pessimism. Instead, he taught the Saints to "greatly rejoice," even though they were "in heaviness through manifold temptations." He counseled them to remember that "the trial of [their] faith" would lead to "praise and honour and glory at the appearing of Jesus Christ" and to "the salvation of [their] souls" (1 Peter 1:6–7, 9). Peter's faith must have been comforting to those early Saints, as it is encouraging to Saints today, who are also "partakers of Christ's sufferings; that, when his glory shall be revealed, [we] may be glad also with exceeding joy" (1 Peter 4:13).

 ## Ideas for Personal Scripture Study

1 PETER 1:3–9; 2:19–24; 3:14–17; 4:12–19

I can find joy during times of trial and suffering.

The period after Christ's Crucifixion wasn't an easy time to be a Christian, and Peter's first epistle acknowledges that. In the first four chapters, you'll notice words and phrases describing hardship: *heaviness, temptations, grief, fiery trial,* and *sufferings* (see 1 Peter 1:6; 2:19; 4:12–13). But you'll also notice words that seem joyful—you may want to make a list of what you find. For example, as you read 1 Peter 1:3–9; 2:19–24; 3:14–17; and 4:12–19, what gives you hope that you can find joy even amid difficult circumstances?

You might also read President Russell M. Nelson's message "Joy and Spiritual Survival" (*Ensign* or *Liahona*, Nov. 2016, 81–84) and look for similarities between what Peter taught and what President Nelson taught. What is it about the plan of salvation and the gospel of Jesus Christ that gives you joy?

See also Ricardo P. Giménez, "Finding Refuge from the Storms of Life," *Ensign* or *Liahona*, May 2020, 101–3.

1 PETER 3:18–20; 4:1–6

The gospel is preached to the dead so they can be judged justly.

One day each person will stand at the judgment bar and "give account to him that is ready to judge the quick and the dead" (1 Peter 4:5). How can God judge all people fairly when their opportunities to understand and live the gospel are so different? Notice how the doctrine that Peter taught in 1 Peter 3:18–20; 4:6 helps answer this question. How do these verses strengthen your faith in God's fairness and justice?

To explore this doctrine further, study Doctrine and Covenants 138, a revelation President Joseph F. Smith received as he pondered these writings of Peter. What additional truths did President Smith learn?

See also Gospel Topics, "Baptisms for the Dead," topics.ChurchofJesusChrist.org.

2 PETER 1:1–11

Through the power of Jesus Christ, I can develop my divine nature.

Do you ever feel that becoming like Jesus Christ and developing His attributes is not possible? Elder Robert D. Hales offered this encouraging thought about how we can develop Christlike attributes: "The attributes of the Savior . . . are interwoven characteristics, added one to another, which develop in us in interactive ways. In other words, we cannot obtain one Christlike characteristic without also obtaining and influencing others. As one characteristic becomes strong, so do many more" ("Becoming a Disciple of Our Lord Jesus Christ," *Ensign* or *Liahona*, May 2017, 46).

Each Christlike quality we develop helps us weave a spiritual tapestry of discipleship.

As you read 2 Peter 1:1–11, ponder the attributes "of the divine nature" listed in these verses. In your experience, how are they "interwoven," as Elder Hales described? How do they build on each other? What else do you learn from these verses about the process of becoming more Christlike?

You might also ponder the "exceeding great and precious promises" God gives His Saints—including you (2 Peter 1:4). Elder David A. Bednar's message "Exceeding Great and Precious Promises" (*Ensign* or *Liahona*, Nov. 2017, 90–93) can help you understand what those promises are and how to receive them.

 ## Ideas for Family Scripture Study and Home Evening

1 Peter 2:5–10. As you read these verses with your family, consider using rocks to help family members visualize Peter's teachings that the Savior is our "chief corner stone." How are we like the "lively [living] stones" that God is using to build His kingdom? What do we learn from Peter about the Savior and our role in His kingdom? What is Peter's message to your family?

1 Peter 3:8–17. How can we "be ready always to give an answer" to those who ask us about our faith? Your family might enjoy role-playing situations in which someone approaches them with a question about the gospel.

1 Peter 3:18–20; 4:6. What can your family do to feel connected to your ancestors? Perhaps you could celebrate deceased ancestors' birthdays by preparing their favorite meals, looking at pictures, or telling stories from their lives. If possible, you could also plan to receive ordinances for your ancestors in the temple (for help, visit FamilySearch.org).

2 Peter 1:16–21. In these verses, Peter reminded the Saints of his experience on the Mount of Transfiguration (see also Matthew 17:1–9). What do we learn from these verses about the teachings of prophets? (see also Doctrine and Covenants 1:38). What gives us confidence to follow our living prophet today?

For more ideas for teaching children, see this week's outline in *Come, Follow Me—For Primary*.

Suggested song: "Family History—I Am Doing It," *Children's Songbook*, 94.

Improving Our Teaching

"Be ready always." Informal teaching moments at home can come and go quickly, so it's important to take advantage of them when they arise. How can you strive to "be ready always" to teach your family members gospel truths and share "the hope that is in you" (1 Peter 3:15) when teaching moments arise? (See *Teaching in the Savior's Way*, 16.)

Even though Peter faced much persecution and opposition, he remained steadfast in his testimony of Christ.

Perfect Love, by Del Parson

1–3 John; Jude

"GOD IS LOVE"

As you read the Epistles of John and Jude, seek inspiration about how you can show your love to God. Record these impressions and act on them.

RECORD YOUR IMPRESSIONS ____

____

____

When John and Jude wrote their epistles, corrupt doctrine had already started leading many Saints into apostasy. Some false teachers were even questioning whether Jesus Christ had actually appeared "in the flesh" (see, for example, 1 John 4:1–3; 2 John 1:7). What could a Church leader do in such a situation? The Apostle John responded by sharing his personal witness of the Savior: "This is the testimony which we give of that which was from the beginning, which we have heard, which we have seen with our eyes, which we have looked upon, and our hands have handled, of the Word of life" (Joseph Smith Translation, 1 John 1:1 [in 1 John 1:1, footnote *a*]). And then John taught about love: God's love for us and the love we should have for Him and all His children. After all, John was a witness of that, too. He had personally experienced the Savior's love (see John 13:23; 20:2), and he wanted the Saints to feel that same love. John's testimony and teachings on love are just as needed today, when faith in Jesus Christ is questioned and false teachings abound. Reading John's epistles can help us face today's adversities with courage, for "there is no fear in love; but perfect love casteth out fear" (1 John 4:18).

Ideas for Personal Scripture Study

1 JOHN; 2 JOHN

God is light, and God is love.

If you were to choose one or two words to describe God, what would they be? In his epistles, John often used the words "light" and "love" (see, for example, 1 John 1:5; 2:8–11; 3:16, 23–24;

4:7–21). As you read the first two epistles of John, ponder the experiences John had with the Savior's light and love. For example, consider what John learned from Jesus's teachings in John 3:16–17; 12:35–36, 46; 15:9–14; 19:25–27. Do you see any similarities between these teachings and what 1 John teaches about the light and love of God? What experiences have taught you that God is light and love?

1 JOHN 2–4; 2 JOHN

"If we love one another, God dwelleth in us."

You will also find words like "abide" and "dwell" repeated throughout John's epistles. Look for these words, especially as you read 1 John 2–4 and 2 John. What do you think it means to "abide" or "dwell" in God and His doctrine? (see 2 John 1:9). What does it mean to you to have God "abide" or "dwell" in you?

1 JOHN 2:24–3:3

I can become like Jesus Christ.

Does the goal of becoming Christlike ever seem too lofty to you? Consider John's encouraging counsel: "Little children, abide in him; that, when he shall appear, we may have confidence . . . [and] we shall be like him" (1 John 2:28; 3:2). What do you find in 1 John 2:24–3:3 that gives you confidence and comfort as a disciple of Jesus Christ? As you study John's epistles, look for other principles or counsel that can help you in your effort to become more Christlike.

See also Moroni 7:48; Doctrine and Covenants 88:67–68; Scott D. Whiting, "Becoming like Him," *Ensign* or *Liahona*, Nov. 2020, 12–15.

1 JOHN 4:12

Has "no man . . . seen God at any time"?

Joseph Smith Translation, 1 John 4:12 clarifies that "no man hath seen God at any time, *except them who believe*" (in 1 John 4:12, footnote *a*; see also John 6:46; 3 John 1:11). The scriptures record several instances when God the Father has manifested Himself to faithful individuals, including John himself (see Revelation 4; see also Acts 7:55–56; 1 Nephi 1:8; Doctrine and Covenants 76:23; Joseph Smith—History 1:16–17).

1 JOHN 5

As I exercise faith in Jesus Christ and am born again, I can overcome the world.

As you read 1 John 5, look for what we must do to overcome the world and gain eternal life. What might overcoming the world look like in your life? You could also find answers and insights in Elder Neil L. Andersen's message "Overcoming the World" (*Ensign* or *Liahona*, May 2017, 58–62).

JUDE 1

"[Build] up yourselves on your most holy faith."

What does Jude 1:10–19 teach you about those who fight against God and His work? What do you learn from verses 20–25 about how to keep your faith in Jesus Christ strong?

Ideas for Family Scripture Study and Home Evening

1 John 2:8–11. To help your family ponder John's teachings, gather in a dark room so family members can experience the difference between walking "in darkness" and walking "in the light." How does hatred cause us to walk in darkness and stumble? How does loving each other bring light into our lives?

1 John 3:21–22. What in these verses increases the "confidence" that we have in God and in our ability to receive answers to our prayers?

Keeping God's commandments helps us overcome the world.

1 John 5:2–3. Are there any commandments that we consider "grievous" or difficult to follow? How does our love for God change the way we feel about His commandments?

3 John 1:4. What does it mean to "walk in truth"? You might take this opportunity to tell family members how you have seen them walk in truth and talk about the joy this brings you. Family members might enjoy writing about or drawing truths they have learned on paper footprints and using them to make a path your family can walk on together.

Jude 1:3–4. Are there any spiritual dangers that have "crept in" to our lives and family? (Jude 1:4). How can we follow Jude's admonition to "earnestly contend for the faith" and resist these dangers? (Jude 1:3). What can we do to ensure that "peace, and love, be multiplied" in our family? (Jude 1:2).

For more ideas for teaching children, see this week's outline in *Come, Follow Me—For Primary.*

Suggested song: "Where Love Is," *Children's Songbook,* 138–39.

Improving Personal Study

Find God's love. President M. Russell Ballard taught, "[The] gospel is a gospel of love—love for God and love for one another" ("God's Love for His Children," *Ensign,* May 1988, 59). As you read the scriptures, make note of evidences of God's love.

Walk with Me, by Greg K. Olsen

Revelation 1–5

"GLORY, AND POWER, BE UNTO . . . THE LAMB FOR EVER"

Consider writing down questions you have about what you read in Revelation. You can then search for answers to your questions or discuss them with a family member or in Church classes.

RECORD YOUR IMPRESSIONS

Have you ever struggled to express to others what you felt during a powerful spiritual experience? Everyday language can feel inadequate to describe spiritual feelings and impressions. Perhaps this is why John used such rich symbolism and imagery to describe his majestic revelation. He could have simply stated that he saw Jesus Christ, but to help us understand his experience, he described the Savior using words like these: "His eyes were as a flame of fire," "out of his mouth went a sharp twoedged sword," and "his countenance was as the sun shineth in his strength" (Revelation 1:14–16). As you read the book of Revelation, try to discover the messages John wanted you to learn and feel, even if you don't understand the meaning behind every symbol. Why might he have compared Church congregations to candlesticks, Satan to a dragon, and Jesus Christ to a lamb? Ultimately, you don't have to understand every symbol in Revelation to understand its important themes, including its most prominent theme: Jesus Christ and His followers will triumph over the kingdoms of men and of Satan.

Ideas for Personal Scripture Study

John's vision teaches about Heavenly Father's plan to save His children.

The book of Revelation can be hard to understand, but don't get discouraged. John's promise may inspire you to keep trying: "Blessed are they who *read*, and they who *hear and understand* the words of this prophecy, and *keep* those things which are written therein, for the time of the coming of the Lord draweth nigh" (Joseph Smith Translation, Revelation 1:3 [in the Bible appendix], emphasis added).

One way to study Revelation is to look for connections to the plan of salvation. This general overview may help you:

- Chapters 5 and 12 describe events in the premortal life.

- Chapters 6–11, 13–14, 16–19 describe mortal life and events in the history of the earth.

- Chapters 2–3, 15, 20–22 describe the Final Judgment and the glory that awaits the faithful.

As you read, ask yourself, "What does this teach me about God's plan? What has God done to help me overcome evil and return to Him? What are His promises to the faithful?"

It might also be helpful to know that Doctrine and Covenants 77 explains some of the symbols used in Revelation. In addition, the Joseph Smith Translation clarifies several passages in Revelation, so check the footnotes and the Bible appendix regularly.

See also Bible Dictionary, "John," "Revelation of John."

REVELATION 1

Jesus Christ is the Living Son of the Living God.

The first chapter of Revelation describes Jesus Christ's appearance to John in a vision. Perhaps you could make a list of everything this chapter says about Jesus Christ, including who He is, what He does for us, and what He is like.

Some things you learn will come from symbols. Ponder what the Lord might be trying to teach you about Himself through these symbols. For example, notice that the Savior calls Himself "the beginning and the ending" and "the first and the last." Why do you think these titles are significant? What do these titles teach you about the Savior?

REVELATION 2–3

Jesus Christ knows me personally and will help me overcome my challenges.

The Savior's words in Revelation 2–3 reveal that He understood the successes and struggles unique to each branch of the Church in John's day. He praised the efforts of the Saints and also warned them of things they needed to change. What do you learn from the Savior's praise and warnings?

The Savior also understands *your* successes and struggles, and He wants to help you. Note the frequent promises He offers to those who overcome. What impresses you about these promises? What might the Lord want you to overcome? What can you do to receive His help?

REVELATION 4–5

Only Jesus Christ could make Heavenly Father's plan possible.

What do you learn about Heavenly Father from Revelation 4 and about Jesus Christ from Revelation 5? Consider what it must have been like when we all realized that Jesus Christ (the "Lamb") would make Heavenly Father's plan possible (the Savior could "open the book, and . . . loose the seven seals" [Revelation 5:5]). Why could Jesus Christ alone do this? How can you show your faith in Him as your Savior?

See also Job 38:4–7; Doctrine and Covenants 77:1–7.

 # Ideas for Family Scripture Study and Home Evening

Revelation 1:20. Why did Jesus compare His Church to candlesticks? (see Matthew 5:14–16). Sing a song about how we can be like a light on a candlestick, such as "Shine On" (*Children's Songbook*, 144).

Revelation 2–3. Pretend John was asked to give a message to your family like the ones he gave to the churches during his time. What would he say is going well? How might you improve?

Revelation 3:15–16. After reading these verses, your family could drink something lukewarm that tastes better hot or cold. What does it mean to be lukewarm spiritually?

Revelation 3:20. Show the picture of the Savior knocking at the door (see the end of this outline) as your family reads Revelation 3:20. Why does Jesus knock instead of just coming inside? Family members could take turns knocking on a door. Then someone else in the family could suggest a way we can "open the door" to the Savior and let the family member in. How would it feel to have the Savior in our home?

Revelation 4:10–11. What does it mean to worship Heavenly Father? What do we know about Him that makes us want to worship Him?

Revelation 5:6, 12–13. Why is Jesus Christ called the "Lamb"? What does this title teach us about Him?

For more ideas for teaching children, see this week's outline in *Come, Follow Me—For Primary*.

Suggested hymn: "Jesus, Once of Humble Birth," *Hymns*, no. 196.

Improving Our Teaching

Encourage questions. Questions are an indication that family members are ready to learn and give insight into how they are responding to what they're being taught. Teach your family how to find answers in the scriptures. (See *Teaching in the Savior's Way*, 25–26.)

Let Him In, by Greg K. Olsen

Revelation 6–14

"THEY OVERCAME . . . BY THE BLOOD OF THE LAMB"

President Boyd K. Packer counseled: "If the language of the scriptures at first seems strange to you, keep reading. Soon you will come to recognize the beauty and power found on those pages" ("The Key to Spiritual Protection," *Ensign* or *Liahona*, Nov. 2013, 27).

RECORD YOUR IMPRESSIONS

Imagine a woman "travailing in birth, and pained to be delivered." Now imagine "a great red dragon, having seven heads and ten horns" hovering over the woman, poised to "devour her child as soon as it was born" (Revelation 12:2–4). To understand these verses of John's revelation, remember that these images represent the Church and kingdom of God and the peril they would face. For the Saints who experienced intense persecution in John's day, victory over evil may not have seemed likely. This victory can also be hard to foresee in a day like ours, when the adversary is at "war with the saints" and has "power . . . over all kindreds, and tongues, and nations" (Revelation 13:7). But the end of John's revelation gloriously shows that good will prevail over evil. Babylon will fall. And the Saints will come "out of great tribulation" with robes of white—not because their robes were never stained but because the Saints will "have washed their robes, and made them white in the blood of the Lamb" (Revelation 7:14).

 Ideas for Personal Scripture Study

REVELATION 6–11

John saw many events of earth's history, especially those of the latter days.

In these chapters you will read about a book with seven seals. If you wonder what that means, you aren't alone. The Prophet Joseph Smith did too. The Lord revealed to Joseph that this book and its seals represent the story of the earth's "temporal existence," with each seal representing a thousand years (see Doctrine and Covenants 77:6–7). You might be interested to know that the events of the first four seals are summarized in John's vision in only eight verses (Revelation 6:1–8). The next three verses describe the fifth seal (verses 9–11). The events of the last two seals take up most of the rest of the book of Revelation. In other words, the main focus of John's vision is the last days—our days. As you read, ponder why it is valuable to know what John wrote about the latter days.

As you read about the events John prophesied of, consider the following suggestions and questions:

- Read Revelation 7 with the work of gathering Israel in mind. What thoughts do you have about this work? (see also Doctrine and Covenants 77:8–11). What do you learn from verses 13–17 about Jesus Christ and those who come to Him?

- What do chapters 8; 9; and 11 teach you about the events of the last days? (see also Doctrine and Covenants 77:12–13, 15). How can we prepare spiritually for these events?

- Revelation 10 tells of a book that an angel gives to John and commands him to eat. What might this symbolize? (see Doctrine and Covenants 77:14).

REVELATION 12–13

The War in Heaven continues on earth.

We don't know a lot about the War in Heaven, but there is a vivid though brief description of it in Revelation 12:7–11. As you read these verses, picture yourself as part of that premortal conflict. What do you learn about how Satan is overcome? (see verse 11).

The war that started in heaven continues on earth, as Satan persists to "make war with [those who] have the testimony of Jesus Christ" (Revelation 12:17). What do you learn from Revelation 13 about how he is waging that war today? How do "the blood of the Lamb" and "the word of [your] testimony" (Revelation 12:11) continue to help you in this war?

See also 1 Nephi 14:12–14; Moroni 7:12–13; Moses 4:1–4; Doctrine and Covenants 29:36–37; Gospel Topics, "War in Heaven," topics.ChurchofJesusChrist.org.

REVELATION 14:6–7

"I saw another angel . . . having the everlasting gospel."

One fulfillment of the prophecy in these verses occurred when Moroni appeared to Joseph Smith and led him to the records that he translated and published as the Book of Mormon. This book contains the "everlasting gospel" that we are charged with preaching unto "every nation, and kindred, and tongue, and people" (Revelation 14:6).

To learn about other angels who have participated in restoring the everlasting gospel, see Doctrine and Covenants 13; 27:5–13; 110:11–16; 128:20–21.

See also "The Restoration of the Fulness of the Gospel of Jesus Christ: A Bicentennial Proclamation to the World," ChurchofJesusChrist.org.

 ## Ideas for Family Scripture Study and Home Evening

Revelation 7:9, 13–15. What can these verses teach us about why we wear white for baptismal and temple ordinances?

Revelation 7:14–17. Consider inviting family members to share their feelings about the Lord's promises in these verses. How can His promises help us when we are in "great tribulation"? (verse 14).

Revelation 12:7–11; 14:6. Some family members might enjoy drawing pictures of the visions described in Revelation. For example, drawing pictures based on Revelation 12 could lead to discussions about the War in Heaven (see verses 7–11). Pictures based on Revelation 14:6 could lead to discussions about the Restoration of the gospel.

After reading Revelation 14:6 together, consider showing pictures of the angel Moroni and of other angels who helped restore the gospel in our day (see the pictures at the end of this outline). Perhaps family members could take turns holding up one of the pictures and sharing reasons they are thankful that angels came "having the everlasting gospel to preach unto [us]."

Revelation 12:11. What might the phrase "the word of their testimony" mean? How do our testimonies of Jesus Christ help us and others overcome Satan?

Revelation 13:11–14. What thoughts do your family members have about the deceiving beast? How do we detect and avoid deceptions we see in the world today?

For more ideas for teaching children, see this week's outline in *Come, Follow Me—For Primary*.

Suggested song: "I Will Be Valiant," *Children's Songbook*, 162.

Improving Personal Study

Immerse yourself in the scriptures. President Russell M. Nelson taught, "Daily immersion in the word of God is crucial for spiritual survival, especially in these days of increasing upheaval" ("Hear Him," *Ensign* or *Liahona*, May 2020, 89). What does "immersion in the word of God" mean to you?

Moroni Delivering the Golden Plates, by Gary L. Kapp; *Upon You My Fellow Servants,* by Linda Curley Christensen and Michael T. Malm (John the Baptist confers the Aaronic Priesthood on Joseph Smith); *Keys of the Kingdom,* by Linda Curley Christensen and Michael T. Malm (Peter, James, and John confer the Melchizedek Priesthood on Joseph Smith); *Vision in the Kirtland Temple,* by Gary E. Smith (Moses, Elias, and Elijah appear to Joseph Smith and Oliver Cowdery).

Christmas

"GOOD TIDINGS OF GREAT JOY"

Consider how pondering the Savior's birth and mission can help bring a spirit of peace and sacredness to the Christmas season.

RECORD YOUR IMPRESSIONS

Why does the birth of a baby bring such great joy? Perhaps because a new baby can be a symbol of hope. There's something about a brand-new life full of possibilities that invites us to ponder what life might hold for that child and what wonderful things he or she will accomplish. Never has this been truer than at the birth of the Son of God, Jesus Christ. Never has there been more hope placed in a child, and never has there been one born with so much promise.

When an angel invited shepherds to seek a newborn child in a manger, he also gave them a message about that child. It was a message of hope—that this baby had come to earth to fulfill a sacred mission. The shepherds made their message "known abroad . . . and all they that heard it wondered at those things which were told them by the shepherds. But Mary kept all these things, and pondered them in her heart" (Luke 2:17–19). Perhaps it would be good to follow Mary's example this Christmas: to ponder in your heart the things you have learned about the Savior this year. How did He fulfill His mission of redemption in the accounts you have read? And more important, how has His mission changed your life? Then you might feel inspired to follow the example of the shepherds: how will you make it "known abroad" what Jesus Christ has done for you?

Ideas for Personal Scripture Study

MATTHEW 1:18–25; 2:1–12; LUKE 1:26–38; 2:1–20

Jesus Christ condescended to be born among us on earth.

Even if you have read or heard the story of the birth of Jesus Christ many times before, study it this time with this thought in mind: "Christmas is not only a celebration of *how* Jesus came into the world but also of knowing *who* He is—our Lord and Savior, Jesus Christ—and of *why* He came" (Craig C. Christensen, "The Fulness of the Story of Christmas" [First Presidency Christmas devotional, Dec. 4, 2016], broadcasts.ChurchofJesusChrist.org).

What do you know about who Jesus Christ was before He was born? (see, for example, John 17:5; Mosiah 3:5; Doctrine and Covenants 76:13–14, 20–24; Moses 4:2). How does this knowledge affect the way you feel when you read about His birth?

What do you know about why Jesus Christ came to earth? (see, for example, Luke 4:16–21; John 3:16–17; 3 Nephi 27:13–16; Doctrine and Covenants 20:20–28). How does this knowledge affect the way you feel about the Savior? How does it affect the way you live?

See also 2 Corinthians 8:9; Hebrews 2:7–18; 1 Nephi 11:13–33; Alma 7:10–13; "The Nativity" (video), ChurchofJesusChrist.org.

1 CORINTHIANS 15:21–26; COLOSSIANS 1:12–22; 1 PETER 2:21–25

Jesus Christ fulfilled His mission and made it possible for me to inherit eternal life.

Although the story of Christ's birth was surrounded by miraculous events, His would be just another birth if it weren't for the great work that He accomplished later in His life. As President Gordon B. Hinckley put it, "The babe Jesus of Bethlehem would be but another baby without the redeeming Christ of Gethsemane and Calvary, and the triumphant fact of the Resurrection" ("The Wondrous and True Story of Christmas," *Ensign*, Dec. 2000, 5).

Gethsemane, by J. Kirk Richards

Evidence of the Savior's divine mission and His powerful love for others is found throughout the New Testament. Which passages or accounts come to your mind? You might look back through this resource or your study journal and review some of the impressions you recorded. You could also read 1 Corinthians 15:21–26; Colossians 1:12–22; 1 Peter 2:21–25 and ponder how the Savior and His work have blessed your life. What do you feel inspired to change in your life? How will you draw on the Savior's power?

 # Ideas for Family Scripture Study and Home Evening

Matthew 1:18–25; 2:1–12; Luke 1:26–38; 2:1–20. How can you celebrate the birth of Jesus Christ with your family? Here are a few ideas, or you can come up with your own:

- Read or act out parts of the Nativity story together.

- Watch the video "The Christ Child" (ChurchofJesusChrist.org).

- Explore some of the resources in the "Jesus Christ" collection in the Gospel Library, especially in the section titled "His Birth (Christmas)."

- Watch a First Presidency Christmas devotional (broadcasts.ChurchofJesusChrist.org).

- Sing Christmas hymns together, or choose neighbors or friends to visit and sing to them (see *Hymns*, nos. 201–14).

- Perform an act of service.

- Ask family members to look for details in the Nativity story that give them ideas for ornaments or decorations they could make to remind them of Jesus Christ.

1 Corinthians 15:21–26; Colossians 1:12–22; 1 Peter 2:21–25. Why are we grateful that Jesus Christ was born? What gifts has He given us? How can we show Him our gratitude? Your family could sing a song that teaches about His mission, such as "He Sent His Son" (*Children's Songbook*, 34–35).

"The Living Christ: The Testimony of the Apostles." If you want to help your family focus on the Savior at Christmastime, perhaps you could spend some time reading and studying together "The Living Christ: The Testimony of the Apostles" (ChurchofJesusChrist.org). Maybe you could memorize passages from "The Living Christ" or look for descriptions of the Savior's life in the New Testament that support statements in it. You could also invite each family member to write his or her own testimony of Jesus Christ and, if so prompted, read it to the family.

For more ideas for teaching children, see this week's outline in *Come, Follow Me—For Primary*.

Suggested song: "Once within a Lowly Stable," *Children's Songbook*, 41.

Improving Personal Study

Look for Jesus Christ. The scriptures teach us that all things testify of Jesus Christ (see Moses 6:62–63), so we should look for Him in all things. As you read the scriptures, consider noting or marking verses that teach you about Him. Take time in the days leading up to Christmas to look for things around you that testify of Jesus Christ.

The Nativity, by Brian Call

Revelation 15–22

"HE THAT OVERCOMETH SHALL INHERIT ALL THINGS"

Sometimes the biggest obstacle to learning is our assumption that we don't need to learn—that we already know. As you read the scriptures, be open to new insights that the Lord wants to give you.

RECORD YOUR IMPRESSIONS

As you may recall, the book of Revelation begins with the Savior declaring Himself to be "the beginning and the ending" (Revelation 1:8). Fittingly, it ends with similar words: "I am . . . the beginning and the end" (Revelation 22:13). But what does that mean? The beginning and the end of what? The book of Revelation powerfully testifies that Jesus Christ is the beginning and end of *everything*—of the great, sweeping drama of human existence and salvation. He is "the Lamb slain from the foundation of the world" (Revelation 13:8). And He is the King of kings who brings an end to wickedness, sorrow, and even death itself and ushers in "a new heaven and a new earth" (Revelation 21:1).

Yet before this new heaven and new earth arrive, there is much for us to overcome: plagues, wars, rampant wickedness—all of which Revelation vividly describes. But Jesus Christ is with us during this part too. He is the "bright and morning star" that shines in the dark sky as a promise that dawn is coming soon (Revelation 22:16). And it *is* coming soon. *He* is coming. Even as He invites us, "Come unto me" (Matthew 11:28), He also comes to us. "I come quickly," He declares. And with hope and faith that has been purified in the fires of latter-day adversity, we answer, "Even so, come, Lord Jesus" (Revelation 22:20).

 # Ideas for Personal Scripture Study

REVELATION 16–18; 21–22

The Lord invites me to flee Babylon and inherit "the holy city."

After witnessing the destruction and perils of the last days, John saw a future day that can be summed up in the Lord's declaration "Behold, I make all things new" (Revelation 21:5). One way to understand what that means is to contrast John's description of Babylon, the symbol of worldliness and wickedness (see Revelation 16–18), with his description of the new Jerusalem, symbolic of celestial glory in God's presence (see Revelation 21–22). The chart below might help you:

Babylon	New Jerusalem
Revelation 16:3–6	Revelation 21:6; 22:1–2, 17
Revelation 16:10; 18:23	Revelation 21:23–24; 22:5
Revelation 17:1–5	Revelation 21:2
Revelation 18:11, 15	Revelation 21:4
Revelation 18:12–14	Revelation 21:18–21; 22:1–2

What other differences do you see?

You might also ponder what it means for you to "come out of" Babylon (Revelation 18:4). What do you find in Revelation 21–22 that inspires you to do so?

REVELATION 20:12–15; 21:1–4

All of God's children will be judged out of the book of life.

Suppose an author offered to write a book about your life. What details or experiences would you want included? If you knew that your future actions would also be recorded, how would you approach your life differently? Think about this as you read Revelation 20:12–15. What do you hope will be written about you in the book of life? How would you describe the Savior's role in your book of life? In your opinion, why is it significant that it is called "the Lamb's book of life"? (Revelation 21:27).

If the thought of standing before God to be judged is uncomfortable for you, consider reading Revelation 21:1–4. Referring to these verses, Elder Dieter F. Uchtdorf has said:

"That Day of Judgment will be a day of mercy and love—a day when broken hearts are healed, when tears of grief are replaced with tears of gratitude, when all will be made right. Yes, there will be deep sorrow because of sin. Yes, there will be regrets and even anguish because of our mistakes, our foolishness, and our stubbornness that caused us to miss opportunities for a much greater future.

"But I have confidence that we will not only be satisfied with the judgment of God; we will also be astonished and overwhelmed by His infinite grace, mercy, generosity, and love for us, His children" ("O How Great the Plan of Our God!," *Ensign* or *Liahona*, Nov. 2016, 21).

How do these truths affect the way you view the Final Judgment? What do these truths inspire you to change in your life?

See also Bible Dictionary, "Book of life."

The Last Judgement, by John Scott

Do these verses mean that there cannot be any additional scripture besides the Bible?

Some people have cited Revelation 22:18–19 as a reason to reject the Book of Mormon and other latter-day scripture. You can find an answer to this objection in Elder Jeffrey R. Holland's message "My Words . . . Never Cease" (*Ensign* or *Liahona*, May 2008, 91–94).

Ideas for Family Scripture Study and Home Evening

Revelation 15:2–4. As your family discusses these verses, which refer to "the song of Moses" and "the song of the Lamb," you might read the song of Moses in Exodus 15:1–19, along with other songs mentioned in the scriptures, like Doctrine and Covenants 84:98–102. Why might those who get "the victory over the beast" (Revelation 15:2) feel like singing songs like these? Perhaps your family could sing a hymn or children's song of praise.

Revelation 19:7–9. Perhaps you could look at wedding pictures from your family history or talk about a time when your family attended a wedding celebration. Why is a marriage a good comparison for the Lord's covenant with His Church? (See also Matthew 22:1–14.)

Revelation 20:2–3. How does 1 Nephi 22:26 help us understand what it may mean for Satan to be "bound"?

Revelation 22:1–4. What might it mean to have the Savior's name "in [our] foreheads"? (Revelation 22:4; see also Exodus 28:36–38; Mosiah 5:7–9; Alma 5:14; Moroni 4:3; Doctrine and Covenants 109:22; David A. Bednar, "Honorably Hold a Name and Standing," *Ensign* or *Liahona*, May 2009, 97–100).

For more ideas for teaching children, see this week's outline in *Come, Follow Me—For Primary.*

Suggested song: "When He Comes Again," *Children's Songbook,* 82–83.

Improving Our Teaching

Follow up on invitations to act. "When you follow up on an invitation to act, you show [your family members] that you care about them and how the gospel is blessing their lives. You also give them opportunities to share their experiences" (*Teaching in the Savior's Way,* 35).

Christ in red robes sitting upon a white horse.